STORM
Selling

STORM
Selling

Navigate your team to sales success!

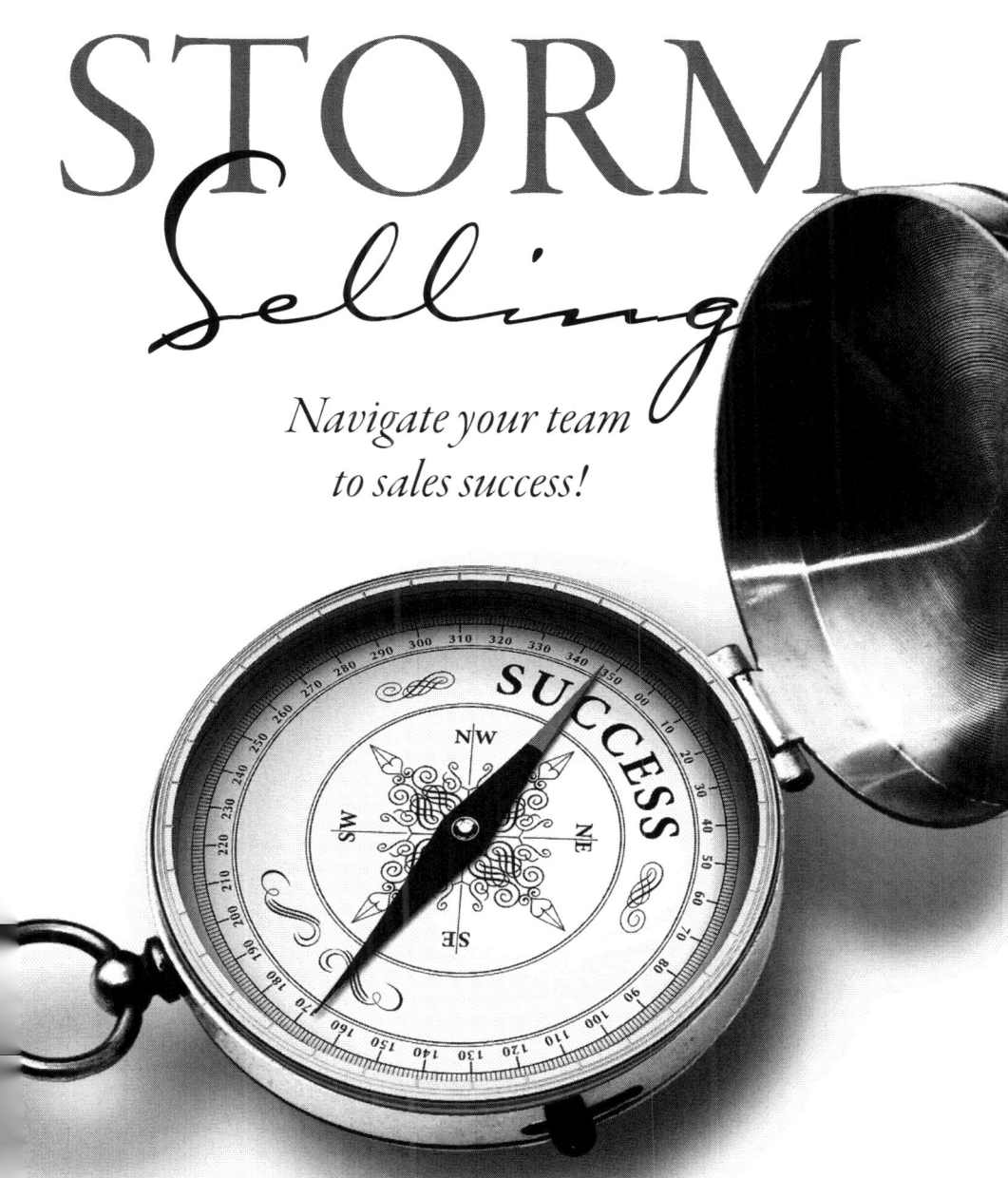

SCOTT McLOUGHLIN

ISBN-13: 978-0-9825259-0-6

www.StormMethod.com

609-279-1911

smcloughlin@att.net

DEDICATION

To Francis Jean

TABLE OF CONTENTS

TABLE OF CONTENTS *(continued)*

ACKNOWLEDGEMENTS

t's hard to believe, but this book is the culmination of forty years of work experiences. One of the important things I learned early on in that forty-year span is that I am, first and foremost, a sales guy. I started out in the typesetting industry, which no longer exists today. I realized fairly quickly that I needed to be in an industry that was forward moving, so I joined a software development firm. My technical skills consisted of the ability to type with two fingers. They may have made fun of my typing but no one made fun of my ability to sell. Every successive job thereafter helped me to hone my craft.

I'd like to begin by acknowledging my clients for being serious about growing their business and for having the courage to reach out to me to help them with that growth. I'd also like to thank them for and staying the course with STORM Method. Of course, my thanks also go out to the many salespeople who have created STORM Plans and participate in STORM Meetings over the years.

Here's a note I got recently from one of these sales representatives:

Hi Scott-

You know how cynical I was about starting storm planning. I didn't think someone with my experience and previous success had to "learn new tricks."
I was cleaning out some old files and came across all of our STORM plans.

We went to the web-based STORM Tool on 3/9/09, 5 months ago; before that we produced 40 separate storm plans.

In crunching the numbers, I learned that of the accounts from my weekly top five, I had a close rate of 37%! When I was in sales management if a salesperson did a 20% close rate, we considered him a crackerjack. 10% close was more the normal. I'm not a great salesman, and I certainly don't work very hard, but I cannot argue with the success of this system.

—Tom Corriveau

I can certainly appreciate the reluctance of salespeople who tend to be the guinea pigs of any company and who are suspicious about any "flavor of the month" idea that comes down the pike. That's why I'm all the more grateful to salespeople like Tom, who gave the system an honest shot and then got in touch to let me know about their success with it.

I'd like to express my thanks to my editor, Brandon Toropov, for all his help with this project. And finally to my wife, our conversations about the educational process and how people learn were invaluable. You were right to stress that all people, need to be "scaffolded" in the learning process. The color coding system was a direct result of those conversations. Helping salespeople and business owners achieve success is my goal and I firmly believe that with STORM Method, you will find that success.

SCOTT MCLOUGHLIN

FOREWORD

'Ve talked to a lot of businesspeople about the STORM System. Once I described it, virtually everyone I've talked to has said, "That's exactly what we need." If you manage a sales team, this *is* exactly what you need. The only question is whether or not you're going to implement it.

Fortunately, the system is very easy to put into practice. Unfortu-

COMPASS POINT:

If you manage a sales team, this is exactly what you need.
The only question is whether or not you're going to implement it.

nately, that's not enough to get some people to change their organization's sales management practices. There are a lot of people out there who know that they *should* make a change in their organization, know exactly *what* change they're supposed to make, and also know that making the change *isn't* going to be all that hard. But they still don't take action. Why? Because they're used to doing things a certain way. They're hooked on the status quo. My feeling is that the majority of those people are eventually going to be the victims, rather than the victors, in the marketplace. A year from now, in this uncertain economy, who knows whether they're going to be in business?

The reality is, I can't implement the STORM System for you; neither can Scott McLoughlin, the visionary sales leader who created it, and neither can anyone else – except for you. My sense is that if you read this book, and if you give the simple, powerful ideas outlined on its pages a fighting chance to catch on in your organization, you'll be very glad indeed that you took action on what you learned here. So will each and every member of your selling team!

If you need any more incentive to get started, consider this: I know for certain that the STORM system works, because I've implemented it successfully in three different companies – each in a different industry – and it's delivered measurable positive results in all three. I have a lubricant distribution business, a manufacturing business, a green, bio-based business – and this system works for all of them. It's is *not* industry specific. In fact, the STORM System has given me the confidence to bring in new salespeople – at a time when my competitors are cutting back!

I think the STORM metric I'm most proud of is this one: In one of the businesses, we went from acquiring two new accounts a week, before implementing STORM, to acquiring *ten* new accounts a week, *after* implementing STORM! I attribute that change directly to the focus on new business development that we were able to instill by following Scott's process, each and every week.

That's what we were able to do. Now it's your turn. Read what follows – and put it into practice!

JEFF HART

President & CEO – Mid-Town Petroleum
Managing Partner – Quest Technology Ventures
Chairman – BioBlend Renewable Resources
Also Serves on the Boards of:
  Ignite Media
  DeJure Solutions

CHAPTER
One

Read This First

I work with a lot of company leaders who are deeply frustrated. Of course, that's probably not much of a surprise. Most of these people are entrepreneurs, and entrepreneurs are never satisfied. But I think it's fair to say that the level of frustration I deal with is both intense - even by the standards of a founder, president, or CEO – and preventable. Their frustration centers on the sales team. My job is to take that frustration away.

Quite frankly, the company leaders I talk with are ready for a change, because they're sick and tired of the results they're getting by sticking with "the way we do it here." They're sick and tired of salespeople and sales departments missing meetings, missing benchmarks, missing reporting deadlines, and missing quota. They are sick of excuses. They are sick of the double-talk they get from both salespeople and the managers who (supposedly) lead their teams. Perhaps most intensely, the corporate leaders I deal with are sick of the finger-pointing that always seems to accompany any significant, sustained performance problem in the sales arena.

COMPASS POINT:

Are you ready for change?

The problem is the reporting system!

The problem is the salespeople who won't use the reporting system!

The problem is the software!

The problem is the lack of software!

The problem is the pipeline management process!

The problem is the lack of a pipeline management process!

The problem is the sales manager's management style!

The problem is the salesperson's attitude!

The problem is that we have too many meetings!

The problem is that we don't have enough meetings!

When "the way we do it here" leads to one or more of the above excuses ... then "the way we do it here" is too expensive.

By the time company leaders get to me, they have heard it all – and they don't want to hear it any more. They bring me in to work with their teams for one reason and one reason alone: They want someone who will take personal responsibility for cleaning up the sales process, hitting the key numbers on a daily, weekly, monthly, and quarterly basis, and (last but not least) making the excuses go away. Forever.

When you get right down to it, that's my job: making the sales team's excuses go away, and replacing those excuses with sales results that make everyone happy.

I'm proud to say that I've been doing just that for over twenty years. And I've done it for hundreds of companies, in just about every industry you can name. I'm not a proud man, but I am a realistic man. The reality-based assessment I offer you, if you're in charge of a sales team, is this: I've got enough repeat clients to support the proposition that what I do

COMPASS POINT:

The one big change I will ask you and your team to implement is to move from being a reactive sales organization to being a proactive sales organization. It will take about 90 days of sustained effort to pull it off.

works. What I share with sales teams really does make excuses a thing of the past, gets sales teams on track, and keeps them on track so they can hit and exceed quota on a regular basis.

Between these covers, you'll find all the tools I use to get my job done and all the insights and advice you need about how to use those tools on behalf of your sales team, your organization, and your own career. I know that what follows can work for you, just as it works for me and the thousands of salespeople I've coached. There's really only one thing you have to embrace up-front for it to work: *be sick and tired enough of the results you're getting from "the way we do it here" to be willing to change what you're doing – sooner rather than later.*

In the next chapter, we'll start to look at how we're going to pull that off.

IMPORTANT: Please do not attempt to implement this system until you have finished this book in its entirety!

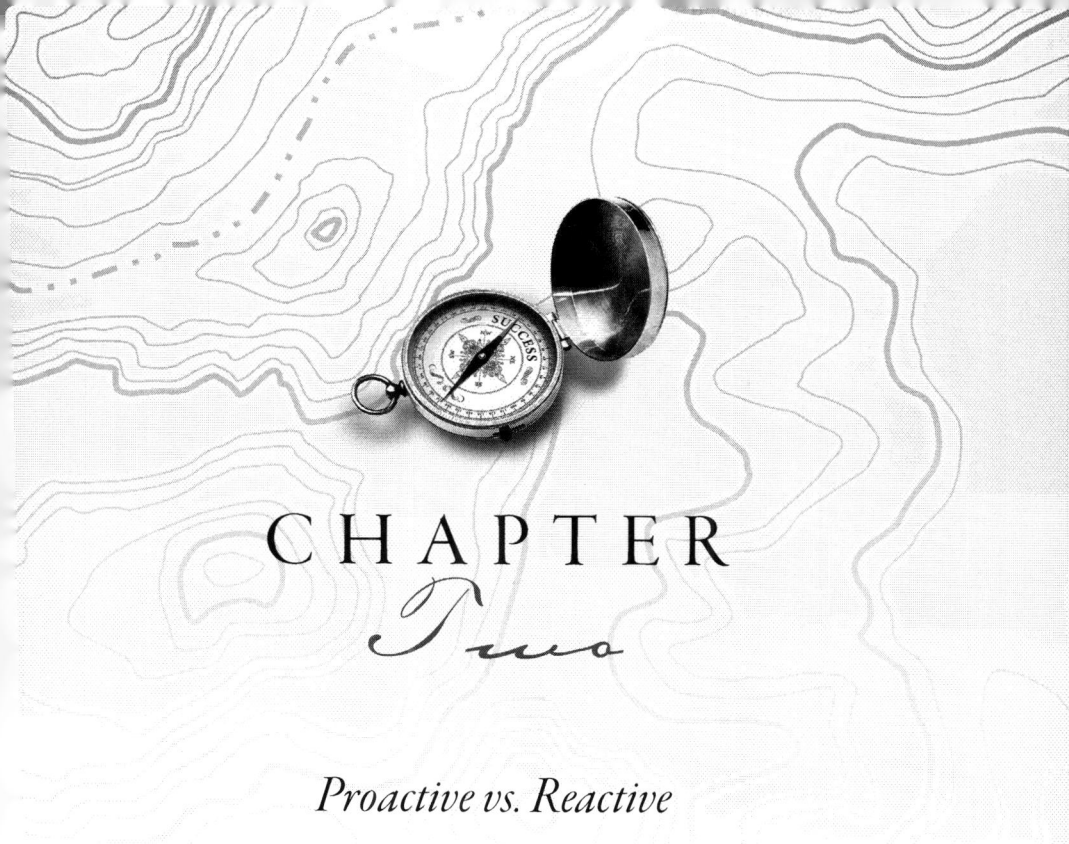

CHAPTER
Two

Proactive vs. Reactive

nce upon a time, there was a drill instructor who woke his recruits up at five in the morning, assembled them in front of the barracks, and told them, "Today, you will run *east* – until you can no longer stand to run anymore." He pointed his team toward the east, told them to start running, and followed along behind them in a Jeep. He found that most people collapsed around mile five; a few people made it to mile eight; one recruit made it to mile ten.

After a couple of weeks of this, the drill instructor changed his routine. He said, "Men, today we're going to start training for a *marathon race* of 26 miles. We're still going to be running east; but this time, I'll let you know when you've hit the one-quarter point, the halfway point, and the three-quarter point – and, of course, I'll also let you know when you've crossed the finish line."

Every single one of his men crossed the finish line.

Some took a great deal longer to do it than others, of course – but nobody bailed out along the way.

WHAT'S THE LESSON HERE?

Behavior that is proactive is more effective, less stressful, and more successful over time than behavior that is reactive.

COMPASS POINT:

Are you asking your team to "run into the sunrise?"

Running into the sunrise until you collapse is essentially *reactive.* It doesn't require much of a plan. Running toward a specific finish line is *proactive* – because you know where you're going and how far along you are at any given moment. As a result, you can pace yourself and create other strategies for getting where you want to go.

Unfortunately, most of the sales teams operating in America today are *reactive.*

In this book, I'm going to give you all the tools your team needs to create a *proactive* sales culture – a culture based on steady, conscious, measurable steps toward a mutually agreed-upon goal. Now, I know there are a lot of people who talk about building such a sales culture, but let's be honest: most of what they preach doesn't actually change the behavior of salespeople. The difference here is that I know, from personal experience, the tools that actually *do* change salespeople's behavior. One tool in particular is essential: *a single piece of paper.*

I didn't say "a pile of single sheets of paper." Knowing as I do that most salespeople have a built-in aversion to paperwork or anything that resembles it, I've built this system around *one* piece of paper per week.

Each salesperson is accountable for completing that single sheet of paper once a week. If they want to fill out more sheets for their own purposes, that's up to them. But outside of expense reports, this is the only sheet they've got formal responsibility for submitting. Some sales managers who are used to making their teams "jump through hoops" need a little time to get their heads around this concept. You should know, before we go any further, that the single sheet of paper is an essential, and non-negotiable, part of this system.

This single sheet of paper becomes the focus of a weekly meeting involving the entire team. It's called a STORM Plan, and the meeting that happens around it is called a STORM meeting. Both are non-negotiable elements of everything that follows.

You'll be learning a great deal more about STORM plans and STORM meetings (as well as a number of other tools and resources) in later chapters of this book. The point to bear in mind right now is that *by making the paperwork simple and manageable and by making the benchmarks so clear that no one could possibly miss them or misunderstand them, you're more likely to make proactive behavior a reality on your team.*

Sometimes sales managers tell me that their team members are "already proactive." My question in these situations is pretty simple: *Do you know the top five opportunities each of your salespeople is working on now and exactly what is supposed to be happening next in each of those conversations?*

COMPASS POINT:

Do you know the top five opportunities each of your salespeople is working on now? Do you know exactly what is supposed to be happening next in each of those conversations?

If the answer is "No," that means your sales team either has a plan and isn't showing it to you or, what's much more likely, your team has no plan and is trying to camouflage that fact.

A lot of "activity" is not what makes a salesperson proactive. A clear, comprehensible *plan*, consistently reviewed and updated, is what makes a salesperson proactive.

The STORM Plan is what will make that proactive step-by-step progress a reality in your team's day-to-day experience.

Perhaps you're wondering – "Why do salespeople need *anything* from us as managers? Why do we have to take the initiative to move them from a low-margin, low-effectiveness, reactive selling routine into a high-margin, high-efficiency, proactive selling routine? Why aren't they proactive on their own?"

Sales managers have been asking that question for decades.

CHAPTER
Three

Why Aren't They Doing This Themselves?

*H*ow did it come to this? Should you really *have to* prompt your salespeople to take the time to put together a weekly plan? Doesn't that seem like something they should be doing on their own? Why do you have to make planning part of a regular meeting?

The best short answer is: Because, somewhere along the way, *you* encouraged your salespeople *not* to plan.

Even though you probably shouldn't *have to* work with salespeople to set up a methodology that helps them present, share, and work their plan ...the reality is that you *do* have to do that. If you're like most sales managers, the reason you have to do that is that you have allowed salespeople to fall into the trap of *magical thinking* about what they do for a living.

Consider this. People tend to *become* salespeople because they like the idea of setting their own income targets – and then hitting those targets. That's one of the big payoffs of this profession: the sky's the limit, and when you achieve big, you and you alone get the reward for doing so. People go into this line of work because they like the idea of controlling their own destiny. What's more, salespeople tend to *stay* salespeople because they enjoy the relative autonomy that this job gives them. Again, they like to call their own shots.

And don't we as sales managers know this?

If we were a salesperson and we hit or exceeded quota, wouldn't we expect the organization to respect our desire for minimal (or nonexistent) supervision? Isn't that reward we expect for the bottom-line result of delivering revenue to the organization?

Sure it is. We would definitely have the expectation that, once we hit or beat the target, people would leave us alone and let us do things our way. And you know what? That expectation would lead us to a pattern, a dynamic, that we would come to expect. Most sales managers are familiar with this pattern, because they buy into it and reinforce it on a regular basis.

In so many words, the salesperson says, **"Leave me alone. I know what I'm doing here."** And, all too often, we buy into that.

COMPASS POINT:
Beware of "magical" sales processes.

Our implied bargain with the salesperson is, "Okay. Tell you what. If you really do know what you're doing, then I, your manager, will, for the most part, leave you alone. *How* you spot, develop, and capitalize on opportunities gets to be your concern. You get to call your own shots. Just hit the numbers."

Basically, we're letting salespeople tell us, "Closing deals is magic, and I'm the one who knows how to do the trick in my territory. Stay out of my way and don't ask too many questions."

And we're pretty much okay with that.

Then the day comes when the salesperson, for whatever reason, *doesn't* hit the numbers he or she is supposed to hit. At that point, the bargain starts to fall apart. We begin to get pressure from our superiors and that in turn makes us put pressure on the salesperson: "Hey, what's going on? What needs to happen next? What are you doing to get back on track?"

And the problem is that the salesperson often doesn't have a very clear answer to those questions. Why? Because the salesperson is too busy feeling threatened by the implied lack of trust that's suddenly emerged in our relationship. Remember, this salesperson got into this line of work because of a desire for independence!

When things go wrong, does the salesperson say to us right out loud, "You know what? I don't actually know what I need to do to get back on track." No. Instead, the salesperson says something like this:

> "Would you relax? I've got a lot of deals in the pipeline and
> I still know what I'm doing. I told you, it's my own special,
> personal procedure I'm working here. Leave me alone – and let
> me work my magic."

And guess what? That's exactly what we do. Even if the person were to ask us for help, the truth is, we might not always know what's supposed to happen next either! Why not? Because nobody has set up much of a plan; nobody has been measuring what's actually happening every week (other than the deals coming in, of course); and nobody has a clear sense of which of the salesperson's activities actually produce sales and which don't. *All we've been doing is counting the deals that actually close!*

Let me ask you this: If you wanted to know what the procedure was for building a quality car and you didn't know anything about that procedure, how much sense would it make to stand at the end of the assembly line and simply count the total vehicles coming off the line? You'd know whether the factory was producing vehicles and you'd know if the factory had *stopped* producing vehicles – but that's all you'd know. If you wanted any more information, you'd eventually have to start tracking what was actually going on inside the factory.

Unfortunately, that's not how we look at our salespeople. We wait for them to do "whatever it is they do" to get back on track so we can get back to counting the deals they close. They're professionals – it's *their* job to get back on track, right?

Maybe – maybe not. Before long, we get pressured by top management *again* about what's really going on and that conversation is no fun. What do we do during that conversation? Well, we don't have a lot of options. We say some variation on the following: "Hey, I told you. I know what I'm doing. I have my own special procedures for managing these people. Leave me alone and let me work my magic with this guy."

Magical thinking is expensive. Inevitably, some important target or other gets missed and the magical excuses stop working. Too much magical excuse-making leads to big problems for everyone, including top management and (alas) us.

Look at it again.

* The reason salespeople don't take on the role of planning is that, all too often, we've given them *permission* not to plan.

* We have accepted their (understandable) desire for autonomy.

* We have accepted their magical explanations to such a degree that we've begun to adopt magical explanations ourselves!

Maybe we're resisting this idea as we read it in black and white. But isn't this what's happened to us at least once in our careers? We've told our salespeople that, as long as they continue to work their mysterious, magical tricks successfully, we won't bug them too much about *how* the

COMPASS POINT:

When we ourselves get into trouble for letting salespeople get away with too much magical double-talk, we sometimes overcompensate for that mistake.

deal actually comes together. We won't try to tell them what they have to do on a consistent basis to create new deals.

There's a common variation on this pattern. When we ourselves get into trouble for letting salespeople get away with too much magical double-talk, have we ever *overcompensated* for that mistake?

Sure we have. We go too far in the opposite direction. We weigh salespeople down with paperwork, meetings, and tracking tools, all of which we know they loathe and will do almost anything to avoid doing. *Why* do they loathe these things and avoid doing them? Not just because these things undercut their sense of independence, though that's certainly bad enough. No, salespeople *also* hate these responses to their "magical thinking" because they *take too damn much time* and *usually don't accomplish anything.*

So what's happened? We've responded to magical thinking by "over-managing" –they know it and we know it.

There is a middle ground between accepting magical thinking and "over-managing" our salespeople. In the next chapter, I'll show you what it is. I'll also show how you can *use* the salesperson's intense desire to "call all the shots" to the organization's benefit ... and to yours.

CHAPTER
Four

Let Them Call Their Shots

uess what? Most salespeople want a system.

They may not say this out loud very often, but it's still true. They would *love* to have a system that delivers the outcomes they want. They just don't want to be micromanaged as they *implement* that system.

You really can put this desire not to be micromanaged to work for your team, your organization, and your career. Here's how: Give salespeople a system, and then make them accountable for a brief weekly summary of what their plan is under that system – and for how the plan is going.

This is not "reporting" in the sense that your team is now used to thinking of reporting. This is not red tape. This is not the stuff they hate and complain about – the endless reports and Excel sheet updates and call reports. This is half an hour a week, *each and every week,* spent getting ready for an hour-long meeting, a meeting that happens *each and every week.*

COMPASS POINT:

Give salespeople a system, and then make them accountable for a brief weekly summary of what their plan is under that system —and for how the plan is going.

The middle ground between "magical thinking" and "over-managing" is a weekly all-team review meeting that happens each and every week, no matter what. That review meeting is based on the one-page STORM plan that each salesperson executes independently and discusses in a team meeting.

The middle ground is giving each member of your sales team the chance to be a hero by creating and executing on the right plan ... and to receive public praise for doing so.

Here's a true story that will illustrate the point. About seventy-five years ago, during a World Series game, the great slugger Babe Ruth walked to home plate with a bat in his hand and pointed to center field. The crowed gasped. Here was the greatest slugger in baseball – actually *forecasting* a home run!

Having "called his shot," Ruth then settled into the batter's box. He stared down the pitcher. He waited for the pitch ... and swung. He connected, and drove the ball deep into the center-field bleachers for a never-to-be-forgotten home run.

Ruth was *proactive.* He called his shot. *Then* he hit the home run.

And people still remember the moment, seventy-five years later.

Do you think Babe Ruth enjoyed himself as he rounded the bases after that home run? I bet he did. He was just like a proactive salesperson who executes on his or her own plan, "points to the fences," and then shares the victory with the rest of the team.

Here's the moral of the story: Salespeople want to be Babe Ruth.

They want to call their own shots, and they want to be the center of attention when calling their own shots actually *works*. This system lets them get all the praise, applause, and positive reinforcement that comes from hitting a big home run – and it doesn't ask them to do anything they hate doing. All it asks them to do is *call their shots* – by creating and executing on their own plan.

So: The strategies in this book give each and every member of our team the tools to *call his or her shot* – and emerge as the hero of the day, the home-run hitter, the Most Valuable Player, when the ball goes over

COMPASS POINT:

Let salespeople be Babe Ruth. Let them call their own shots.

the fence. No, the people on your team won't hit it out of the park every single time. (Babe Ruth didn't do that either, by the way.) But when they *do* hit the ball out of the park, it will be because they've used the tools we've given them, set up their own measurable process, and executed on their own plan. And once that happens, they'll want to get back in the batter's box and do it all again.

That's not all! When our salespeople hit the ball out of the park, we'll be able to tell our superiors exactly *why it happened* and what that salesperson's doing to make sure it happens again – sooner, rather than later.

If what you've read thus far is intriguing enough for you to consider making a change in the way you're currently interacting with your sales team ... read on.

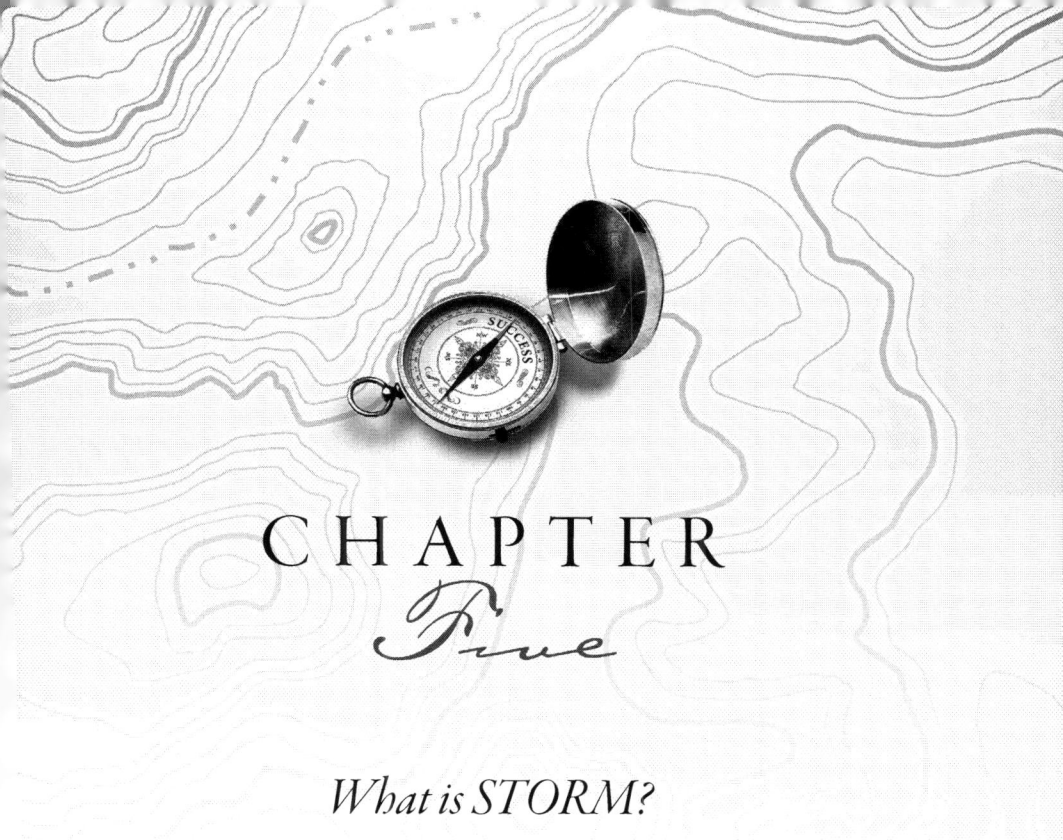

CHAPTER
Five

What is STORM?

*P*erhaps at this stage you're saying to yourself, "It all sounds very interesting, but why on earth is it called a STORM plan, and how is that kind of plan different from any other kind of plan my salespeople have been asked to put together?"

Let's take those two important questions in order. First of all, the STORM plan has that name because the word STORM serves as an acronym for the *five critical elements* that we want our salespeople to habitually notice, track, and, eventually, strategize their work around – week in and week out. Here's how those five elements break down:

The S in STORM stands for SPECIFIC ACTIVITIES. These are what I call Key Performance Indicators, or KPIs. Each member of your team will report what *actually happened* with each of the KPIs during the week just past. If one of the KPIs you're measuring is "dials," and the salesperson made six dials to reach new prospective buyers in the week just past, then that salesperson is going to write the number "six" on the STORM plan and is going to be ready to discuss that number with the group. The KPIs you choose to measure must fit your team like a glove. What makes sense for one team to measure doesn't necessarily make sense for another team operating in a different industry, selling to a different kind of buyer, or possessing a different level of experience.

The T in STORM stands for TOP FIVE. Here, the salesperson identifies his or her top five selling opportunities for the coming week. If the salesperson doesn't *have* at least five opportunities to pursue in the week to come or can't identify those five opportunities, that's obviously cause for concern.

The O in STORM stands for OTHERS WHO CAN HELP. In this category, the salesperson identifies some *person* or specific *group of people* who can help him or her either to move a deal forward or to initiate a new selling opportunity. We're *not* asking the salesperson to keep feuds and rivalries alive by complaining about someone else's perceived shortcomings. The idea here is to focus positively and proactively on people within the organization who can help make something good happen over the next week. The request should connect to a time and date: "I need Jim the help me out on a conference call with a client on Tuesday morning at 10:00, if he's available then."

The R in STORM stands for RESOURCES NEEDED. This is a specific request for support, administrative assistance, or information that the salesperson doesn't currently have access to. It differs from OTHERS WHO CAN HELP, above, because it doesn't have an individual's name or a group of individual names attached to it. For instance: "If anyone has referrals that connect to the banking industry, I'd like to be able to use them for a group of proposals I'm putting together." Or: "I think it's taking us too long to approve or deny credit applications. Right now, we don't let people know what's happening on their application for at least two weeks. Is it possible we could get that down to one week?"

The M in STORM stands for MOVEMENT PROJECTED. In this part of the meeting, salespeople will project what *will* happen with one particular selling opportunity by the time the next STORM meeting rolls around – and they will also be prepared to discuss what actually *did* happen with the opportunity they placed in this slot last week. For both the projection about the coming week and the "reality check" about the week just past, the focus will be on *measurable forward movement in the sale cycle*.

Whether the salesperson is talking what *will* happen in the coming week or what *did* happen in the week that just ended, there is always a danger that a fascinating *story* will emerge. We're not looking for stories.

COMPASS POINT:
We're not looking for stories. We're looking for meaningful benchmarks in the selling cycle.

We're looking for meaningful benchmarks in the selling cycle.

Here's what a story sounds like: "I had a great conversation with Joe So-and-So last Tuesday. It looks like he's going to be doing something with us within the next four to six weeks."

Here's what meaningful benchmarks in the selling cycle sound like:

"This week, I project that I will set up my first face-to-face meeting with Joe So-and-So."

"I gave an in-person presentation to so-and-so based on three previous discussions and will get a decision tomorrow."

"I project that I will close the deal this week and get the signed contract."

As you can see, the MOVEMENT the salesperson tracks or projects is *not* a good story that happens to involve a prospect. Rather, it is tangible evidence that the deal is further along this week than it was last week.

The MOVEMENT the salesperson tracks or projects may look big or small to you, but whenever it moves a deal forward, it is cause for group celebration. *Do not just celebrate the close!* Celebrate every step along the way toward the sale.

Those are the five critical elements; you'll be getting very familiar with them as we go forward. I'll be going into much more detail about each one, as well as how to keep your team's attention focused on all five, in later chapters of this book. What I want you to remember now is this: When someone uses the five STORM elements to establish priorities for the week ... *that person has a PLAN for the week!*

Of course, there is probably no such thing as a *perfect* plan for the week, the quarter, or the year ... but I think you'll agree that *having* a plan is much better than *not* having a plan. What's nice about STORM is that salespeople are far more likely to buy into setting *this* kind of a plan than almost any other.

Why? Well, that brings us to our second big question: "What makes this plan different from the other plans salespeople may have encountered?" **This kind of plan is different because this plan isn't painful!** I'll show you why in the next chapter.

CHAPTER
Six

Why This Plan Isn't Painful

*S*alespeople avoid planning because they are used to thinking of planning as painful.

The question is: *Why* do they think of planning as painful? I've got a theory. It's because, most of the time, salespeople haven't really been asked to plan in the first place. They've been asked to do something else entirely. They've been asked to file *reports*, often about things that everyone knows don't make any difference anyway.

* "How much face time did you spend with live C-level prospects in the widget industry over the past forty-five days? How much face time will you promise to spend with these people over the next forty-five days?"

23

* "How many dials did you make between four-fifteen p.m. and five-fifteen p.m. last Thursday? Didn't you write that down? You were supposed to. How many dials will you make during the same time slot next Thursday?"

* "What's your total wallet share within complex accounts on the Upper West Side? You don't know? You're supposed to. What should it have been? What will it be next quarter?"

Who wants to answer questions like that every week? Not me. If you're honest, you'll admit that you're not very eager to answer those kinds of questions either – so you really shouldn't be surprised to learn that your sales team isn't eager to answer them. It's painful to wrap your

COMPASS POINT:
Don't make your salespeople answer pointless questions.

head around those kinds of questions! And all their strange variations are just as painful for your team.

Answering those questions doesn't really constitute planning. So we're not going to ask the salespeople who report to us to bother with those kinds of questions anymore.

When salespeople track and strategize the *right* things – namely, the five STORM elements I just shared with you – salespeople come to realize that planning isn't painful at all. What *was* painful, they realize, was being held accountable for poorly designed, poorly executed, or poorly administered *reporting systems*.

Once the team gets out of the habit of wasting time, effort, and energy on those systems, and into the habit of using the STORM System (which takes about 90 days), they realize something important. They conclude that planning is a lot less like filling out your tax forms in early April after having put it off for three and a half months and a lot more like Babe Ruth pointing to the fence before hitting a mammoth home run to center field.

Planning is proactive, not reactive. Planning is focused on specific goals and short-terms actions that support those goals. Planning gives you benchmarks that tell you whether you've been getting closer to the goal or further away from it.

If your reporting system isn't delivering that – you're going to stop asking your people to invest time in it.

The big difference between systems that hurt and systems that don't hurt is this: With planning, salespeople actually *know where the finish line is.* They're not being asked to run east until they collapse!

Success in sales means knowing where the finish line really is and, by extension, knowing where the halfway-there and quarter-of-the-way-there marks really are. Once salespeople realize that a *very modest* time investment, week in and week out, will get them that information, they will start buying into the system. That's a promise!

The kind of information the STORM System gives salespeople is the kind they want.

This is not a "reporting system" that yields information designed to help management "keep tabs on people." It's a real, live planning tool that keeps people from having to swallow an elephant in a single sitting. *Salespeople would rather eat the elephant one bite at a time* – just like everyone else would.

I've worked at a lot of startups, and I can tell you from personal experience that it is a whole lot easier to recruit and keep good salespeople if you can give them a workable planning tool – as opposed to a "reporting system." When they know they can use the planning system to get to where they want to go, they tend to stick around!

The STORM System compensates for the challenge that's most common in this profession. That challenge is not the economy; it's not the competition; it's not the prospect who decided not to buy. It's our own lack of a plan.

COMPASS POINT:

Most sales managers don't really create a plan.
They end up creating "reporting systems" instead.

Let's be frank: Salespeople and (ssh!) sales managers are usually a whole lot better at selling than they are at creating a sales plan. Who cares *why* this is true – it's true! As a result, most sales managers don't really create a plan, and they end up relying on "reporting systems" instead. That's backward thinking: It leaves us not knowing how we got into the mess we're in, but with reams of data proving that we really are in a mess. What's even worse is this: reliance on a "reporting system," instead of a solid proactive plan, makes salespeople, and sales teams, focus on *cutting price* in order to close deals and make up lost ground!

By contrast, when they've bought into a real plan, one that they've built with your input, one that they execute on week in and week out and are ready to discuss with you once a week, the members of the team are less likely to have ground to make up – and much *more* likely to focus on a deal's *profitability.*

If that's what you want, and I'm betting it is, you've probably got one big remaining doubt about all this. It probably sounds something like this: "You said they have to do this every week. It all sounds great -- but I know my team. I don't think my people will actually implement this system – or any system – week in and week out."

Surprise, surprise: If you follow the launch plan I'm about to share with you, they *will* buy into this system and make it part of their weekly routine! I'll show you why in the next chapter.

CHAPTER
Seven

Ten Reasons Your Salespeople Will Buy In

G ive me ninety days of honest effort, based on what follows in this book, and I will make believers out of every one of your team members.

Even though some of your people may not buy in to the STORM program initially, they all *WILL* buy into it eventually – if you, the manager, will only commit to implementing the program consistently,

COMPASS POINT:

Commit to implementing the program consistently, week in and week out, for three straight months.

week in and week out, for three straight months.

Here are the ten big reasons your people will buy into this.

1. **They'll realize that STORM is now a fact of life and it's not going away.** If you follow the system I'm going to be sharing with you, the STORM meeting will become a consistent part of your company's culture. Once your topmost management makes this system a priority ... and once you make it a priority ... the sales team will, too.

2. **They'll quickly realize you're not asking them to do more reporting, but less.** The most common reaction to the STORM program sounds like this: "It's only one sheet. I thought I was supposed to be doing a whole bunch of reporting to make this work. This is great." When they find out that they're actually freeing up their own time to sell ... they start looking for reasons to make this system work.

3. **Your best salespeople will realize that this is their chance to have "fifteen minutes of fame."** Although some of your more accomplished people may initially be resistant to STORM meetings, they'll soon see that these gatherings give them the chance to prove that they really do know what they're doing, and to show the "B" team a thing or two about how they ought to be selling.

4. **Your up-and-coming salespeople will realize this is their chance to pick up best practices quickly.**

STORM meetings give people the chance to share what actually worked. Your new people will want to act on this opportunity to compress their learning curve.

5. **Everybody gets a (brief) chance to complain.** No, STORM meetings are not "whining sessions" and they aren't about assigning blame. They are, however, an important public opportunity to raise grievances that deserve management's attention. As long as the complaint is concise and relevant, it's fair to bring it up in the STORM meeting. Salespeople like that. It gives them an outlet they didn't have before.

6. **The meeting is a great equalizer.** Everyone gets measured according to the same metrics. Everyone is accountable for performance in the same areas. Everyone is using the same vocabulary. This builds rapport among team members and improves communication with management. These are outcomes everyone likes.

7. **Before long, salespeople notice that their sales cycles really are getting shorter.** This is the most common, and most easily measurable, benefit of the STORM System. It's also the primary reason people bring me in to work with their sales teams. If salespeople play by these very simple rules, they don't have to wait as long to pick up their commission checks. They *love* that.

8. **Salespeople also notice that their deals are more
    profitable – both for the organization and their own
    personal bottom line.** Not only do salespeople love
    wasting less time and getting a better payback on the time
    they spend selling – *top management* loves the resulting
    improvement in margins.

9. **Salespeople start acting like they're running their
    own business.** Once they start implementing this system
    and taking on accountability for their own results, they
    basically *are* running their own business. They begin to
    look forward to talking about that business once a week.

10. **Deep down, salespeople have always been looking for a
    little bit of help in setting up and executing their sales
    plan.** They may not say this to you out loud, of course,
    but it's a reality, nonetheless. Once you give them a way to
    plan effectively, a way to get good feedback on their plan
    from their peers and from you, and a chance to talk about
    their plan – they'll stick with the system.

Each of your salespeople will probably have different responses to
the STORM program at first. Some people may take a little bit longer
to buy into it than others. Experience has shown, however, that if you
are proactive and consistent enough to make the program a part of the
working environment for three solid months, you won't have to worry
about whether the team will actually use it after that. The short weekly
meetings and the personalized one-page plans will be part of your team's
working culture. When you bring new salespeople on, you'll see your

own team members stepping up to explain to the newcomer "how we really do things here."

Let me share one more thought on "making it stick." Every team has "water-cooler discussions" – you know, those informal sessions where people share how they feel about what's really going on. Once you've implemented the STORM System, you'll find that these "water cooler" topics are much more likely to be about how to *make* things work, rather than who's responsible for things *not* working. This is the ultimate reinforcement tool!

COMPASS POINT:
Make STORM "how we really do things here."

CHAPTER
Eight

If It Ain't Broke, Don't Fix It

efore we look at the heart of the system, the STORM plan, I want to take just a moment to share one of the most common management mistakes in implementing this plan.

The mistake is this: Trying to make the STORM plan your salespeople fill out more complicated than it is meant to be.

What you're about to master is the engine of the whole system. It's

COMPASS POINT:
Don't make the STORM plan more complicated than it is meant to be.

been field-tested with hundreds of sales teams in dozens of industries. If you try to "repair" the engine before you even turn on the car, I can assure you that the car won't run! This engine ain't broke - so please, please, please don't try to fix it.

The initial response I get from a lot of sales managers sounds like this: "That's all it is? It's too simple to work." I promise you - it's not too simple to work! It works because it *is* so simple. Don't try to modify its basic structure. Don't try to expand it. Yes, there are some modifications you'll need to make in order to customize the system for your team. I'll show you exactly how to do that. *The core principles, however, and the basic structure of the plan must not be modified!*

For instance: The STORM plan is designed as a single-page system. Do not try to turn it into a two-page, three-page, or four-page system. It won't work. Your sales team will push back. Keep it simple.

For instance: The vocabulary I use on the STORM plan is so basic that anyone, at any skill level, can quickly start using it. Do not try to change the terminology around or import the product training manual into the form. It won't work. People will stop using it if they don't understand it. Keep it simple.

For instance: You'll notice that the STORM plan asks salespeople to identify their **top five** opportunities for the coming week. The number five is the right number, and it has been field tested extensively. Don't change it! Some sales managers have insisted that a brief list of five opportunities is not enough information for them to make a meaningful assessment. Wrong! Others have assumed that a section where salespeople summarize the "top ten" opportunities must be twice as good as a section where salespeople summarize their top five opportunities. Wrong!

Remember, you're not assessing this one STORM plan from this salesperson- you're assessing a series of STORM plans from this salesperson, each and every week. You'll have plenty to analyze, if you stick with the system. If you start asking your salesperson to identify ten or fifteen opportunities, that salesperson will start thinking of the STORM plan as the one thing it was never meant to be: homework!

If the members of your sales team wanted to do more homework, they would have enrolled in a community college. As it stands, they showed up at your company. So don't give them homework. Give them a single sheet that respects their time, helps them focus on what really works, and lets them get back to what you're paying them to do: Sell!

Have I got your solemn word that you won't try to complicate, expand, or otherwise mess around with the STORM plan you'll be asking the members of your sales team to fill out and discuss each week? If so, let's take a look at that plan now. **If not, stop reading and give the book to someone who will actually implement the system!**

CHAPTER
Nine

The STORM Plan: An Overview

*E*ach and every week, in anticipation of a one-hour meeting or conference call, your people will spend a *maximum* of forty-five minutes completing a one-page planning sheet that looks very similar to this.

Each and every week, in anticipation of a one-hour meeting or conference call, your people will spend a maximum of forty-five minutes completing a one-page planning sheet. You will persistently, but tactfully remind your people that this preparatory time is mandatory, not optional, and is part of a cultural change -- a new routine that emphasizes planning, practice and preparation as part of the weekly cycle. As baseball Hall of Famer Brooks Robinson once said, ""If you're not practicing, somebody else is, somewhere, and he'll be ready to take your job."

The sheet the members of your team will be filling out each week looks very similar to this.

	% Time Servicing Existing	% Time Selling Existing	% Time Firefighting	% Time Prospecting	# New Customers/Gallons
STORM *Method*					
	Ideal Time is 5-10%	Ideal Time is 40%	Ideal Time is 5-10%	Ideal Time is 40%	

Name: _____   Territory: _____

This Week's #1 Opportunity

This Week's #1 Success

Others Who Can Help

Resources Needed

Top 5 Prospective Accounts

Start Date	Start Date	Company Name	Decision Maker(s)	Product(s)/ Services	This Week's Positive Results	Road Blocks	Next Week's Vision and Goals

In fact, the sheet your team fills out will look *exactly* like the one you just saw – with one possible exception. You'll learn what that possible exception is in just a moment.

Let's do a quick review of each of the elements of the weekly plan your team will be putting together for you. As we've already seen, there are five parts of the STORM plan.

The S in STORM stands for SPECIFIC ACTIVITIES. These are metrics that reflect *what each member of your team actually did this week.* This part of the plan represents the only possible change you will want to make to the sample form I shared with you in this chapter. Each team's Key Performance Indicators, or KPIs, must be unique. In a later chapter, I'll give you some examples of the kinds of KPIs you will want to select for measurement based on the kind of team you are leading. I'll also give you some advice on revising this part of the plan for your team over time.

Note: Activity on KPIs will determine your team's weekly, quarterly, and yearly performance. These metrics are the key to making the whole STORM System work, and as a result, they're the element of the STORM plan that I'll be discussing with you, the manager, in the most depth.

The T in STORM stands for TOP FIVE. In this part of the STORM plan, each of your salespeople will write down a few details about his or her top five selling opportunities for the coming week. Your people must be prepared to talk about five – and only five – such opportunities. A little later on in the book, I'll explain what constitutes an opportunity, what doesn't, and what you should do to help salespeople who don't yet *have* five real-world opportunities to pursue.

The O in STORM stands for OTHERS WHO CAN HELP. This part of the STORM plan is where your people identify some *person* or specific *group of people* who may be able to help them to move a deal forward or to initiate a brand new selling opportunity. Later on, I'll give you some examples of what kinds of help you as the manager should be prepared to offer to the members of your team. I'll also give you some ideas about who else in your organization may be able to pitch in.

The R in STORM stands for RESOURCES NEEDED. Here, the members of your team will make specific requests for resources they don't currently have access to. If you're thinking that this part of the STORM plan gives your team the opportunity to complain about things, you're absolutely right. I'll explain why you *must* give them the opportunity to complain during each STORM meeting when it's their turn to discuss RESOURCES NEEDED.

The M in STORM stands for MOVEMENT PROJECTED. As you'll recall, this is a projection for what is *going to happen in the coming week* with a particular selling opportunity. Next week, the team member will be accountable for discussing whether or not what he or she predicted actually took place. If there was no forward movement in the deal that the salesperson identified, the salesperson should acknowledge the discrepancy and share a different experience from the week past about a particular deal that moved forward. For instance, "I closed ABC Company," or "I set an appointment to meet for the first time with the president of XYZ." If *nothing* happened that week to move any deal forward, the salesperson must say so openly and be willing to discuss this during the meeting!

All five of these elements, without exception, must appear on the STORM plan you ask your team to fill out every week.

All five of these elements, without exception, must appear IN THIS ORDER on the sheet your team receives.

All five of these elements must be presented WITH THESE NAMES and no others.

COMPASS POINT:

All five of the STORM elements must appear on the STORM plan you ask your team to fill out every week.

In the chapters that follow, I'll go in-depth on each of the five elements of the STORM plan that will be the focus of your team's weekly meetings.

IMPORTANT REMINDER: Please do not attempt to hold those meetings until you have finished this book in its entirety!

CHAPTER
Ten

Specific Activity: Leading Indicators and Lagging Indicators

The first and most important topic of conversation that each member of your team will discuss during his or her "turn" of the STORM meeting falls into the category called SPECIFIC ACTIVITY.

During this part of the meeting, your salespeople *must* discuss quantifiable sales activities that you all know ahead of time will be measured and discussed as part of the weekly team discussion. No one gets to say, "I didn't know this was going to be on the test!" KPIs are *always* on the test!

I'll give you some specific examples of what the metrics might be for your team in just a moment, but for now, what I'd like you to bear in mind is that this part of the discussion is all about things that can be *counted and measured.*

Again: It's not about interesting stories. It's not about things that almost happened this week, but didn't. It's not about what's probably going to happen *next* week and what the numbers will probably look like then. This part of the meeting is about what *actually* happened and can be counted over the past week.

> **COMPASS POINT:**
> *This part of the discussion is all about things that can be counted and measured.*

The members of your sales team are responsible for *self-reporting* and *self-monitoring* when it comes to the SPECIFIC ACTIVITY discussions. It's not your job as manager to confirm that the numbers they're giving you are correct or verifiable. Some sales managers have a big problem with this part of the STORM System. They ask me, "How do you know whether members of the team are lying?" The only meaningful answer is: "You don't ... *but.*" As in: You don't know whether people are lying about their SPECIFIC ACTIVITY, *but* the people who do will eventually reveal themselves over time if you implement the system impartially, week in and week out, the way it's meant to be implemented. You don't know whether people are lying about their numbers, *but* their colleagues will eventually call them on it if they are. You don't know whether people are lying about their numbers, *but* most people won't and the few who do probably won't be on your team for very long anyway.

The best assumption by far, from all kinds of vantage points, is that the salesperson you're talking to during the STORM meeting is responsible enough to monitor and report his or her numbers responsibly. Any other assumption leads to problems.

The SPECIFIC ACTIVITIES you'll be discussing during this part of the meeting are also known as Key Performance Indicators. No one set of Key Performance Indicators is right for every sales team and it's very likely that the most important Key Performance Indicators for your team will change over time. With that much said, it's possible that you might decide to ask your people to measure the following during any given week.

TOTAL DIALS (where "dial" means picking up the phone to call an individual in an attempt to generate revenue and can only apply to one person called during a single 24-hour period).

TOTAL CONVERSATIONS (where "conversation" means a voice-to-voice discussion with a decision maker or someone we believe to be a decision maker).

TOTAL FACE-TO-FACE MEETINGS (where "face-to-face meeting" means a physical appointment with a decision maker).

TOTAL SALES (where "sale" means you get a purchase order).

I'm going to spend several chapters on the SPECIFIC ACTIVITY portion of the meeting, but I think the most important piece of advice to share with you about this element is this: *Reward your team for focusing on leading indicators first. Don't let them distract you with discussions of lagging indicators.*

Leading indicators are the measurable activities that actually drive your team's sales process. Lagging indicators, by contrast, are the *results of* those leading indicators. For instance, if we were measuring DIALS, CONVERSATIONS, FACE-TO-FACE MEETINGS, and TOTAL SALES, which *one* element would be the leading indicator, the activity that makes everything else happen?

COMPASS POINT:

Each week, you must make sure you are spending most of your time in the SPECIFIC ACTIVITY portion of the conversation, measuring and discussing of each team member's LEADING indicators. You will then move on to a very quick review of the LAGGING indicators.

Of course: It's the dials. For this team, everything begins when someone picks up the phone. If your people stop making dials, there will eventually be no conversations, meetings, or sales to discuss. If they stop making dials, they're in trouble. That's the part you're going to spend most of your time looking at.

In other words: don't get too distracted by the deals that are closing -- whether you like the number of deals the salesperson is reporting or you don't like that number. And don't get too distracted by what happens right *before* a deal closes either. *Do* focus your time, energy, and attention during this part of the discussion on the activities *without which you know for sure there will be no more deals.*

48

CHAPTER
Eleven

Specific Activities --- What They Aren't

*C*ongratulations! You know now how you will open the discussion with each member of your sales team: with a discussion of SPECIFIC ACTIVITIES. You also know that you'll put special priority on measuring the LEADING INDICATORS that connect to those activities.

Now it's time for me to make a prediction.

I predict that, for the first couple of times you conduct this meeting, at least a few members of your team will attempt, with great persistence and commitment, to talk about something *other than* their leading indicators during the opening phase of your team meeting.

I predict that the "something else" they will so desperately want to talk about will fall into one of two very clear categories. They'll either want to talk about *lagging* indicators, for instance, the number of sales they closed, and then skip the discussion of leading indicators entirely *or* they'll want to talk about an activity I call "firefighting" and skip any discussion of leading *or* lagging indicators.

"Firefighting" is something salespeople love to do and love to talk about. In fact, it's something they will end up spending vast amounts of time doing, sometimes to the exclusion of just about everything else they should be doing. Left to their own devices, they might spend 50-60% of the selling week on "firefighting." So that's what they're going to want to talk about. "Firefighting," however, is not what *we* want to talk about or reinforce during this critical opening portion of the meeting.

Now you're wondering: What is "firefighting?"

Basically, firefighting is addressing unexpected problems within an existing account (or even a promising new lead) – *without* making any measurable progress toward some new revenue-producing commitment

COMPASS POINT:
Firefighting is addressing unexpected problems with prospects or customers – with no expectation of generating new revenue.

from the prospect or customer. Firefighting is putting out fires that the customer or prospect identifies for us, typically at the last possible minute. It's also known as "servicing the account."

Whatever we call it, firefighting is *not* asking some variation on this question: "What's the next good project for us to work on together?" It's not new revenue.

The key word here is "new." If the activity in question doesn't connect to some *new* opportunity for a *new* commission check, it's "firefighting," no matter how clearly it may be connected to a customer's desires. And we're not going to waste time or energy talking about it at length during the STORM meeting – despite the fact that this is almost certainly what your team *wants* to talk about.

So for instance, let's say you open the meeting, and you ask your first salesperson to talk about the SPECIFIC ACTIVITIES that got him or her measurably closer to producing revenue that week. You hear the first salesperson start talking about a two-hour-long conference call that he *had* to take part in, in order to keep Important Customer X from deserting to the competition. This call was not about a new project – it was about holding on to an existing project. Your representative starts to replay all the high and low points of the call and explains how he saved the day.

At that point, you have to be ready to step in and redirect the conversation. *This is not what the STORM meeting is about.*

Do not let your team spend its time, effort, and energy discussing that marathon conference call. *That's not what you're here for.* Neither are calls to current customers where we ask them how the wife is, how the kids are, or how the dog is. Technically, that's "firefighting" too – it's just happening before the fire breaks out. If the salesperson didn't ask about new business, it doesn't count as a SPECIFIC ACTIVITY.

Establish whether any of the SPECIFIC ACTIVITIES took place during the salesperson's week. If any did, look at the *leading indicators* first. If none did, move on to the next person. Don't get distracted by stories about "firefighting."

COMPASS POINT:

If the salesperson didn't ask about new business, it doesn't count as a SPECIFIC ACTIVITY.

CHAPTER
Twelve

Specific Activities: The KPI Commandments

nly you can determine the Specific Activities, or Key Performance Indicators, your team should be measuring and discussing
each week.

Sometimes my clients ask me to give them a single definitive list,

COMPASS POINT:

Customize the KPIs to your team.

based on my work with other teams, that will work for every sales team
in their company. Unfortunately, this is impossible. Every team is unique

and requires a customized list of Specific Activities for weekly discussion. This is one area of sales management where one size definitely *does not* fit all. It is likely that you will change the KPI mix over time based on the experience level and recent achievements of your team.

Here's the next best thing to the "definitive" Specific Activities list: A list of reliable principles for creating your own list. Follow these "commandments," and you'll be fine.

TEN KPI COMMANDMENTS

1. All the Specific Activities must be measurable in terms of real activity numbers and/or real time spent. If something cannot be expressed in terms of a number, it does not belong in this part of the meeting.

2. None of the Specific Activities should be tracked by any means other than *self-reporting* on the part of the salesperson in question; none should be difficult to track.

3. At least one of the Specific Activities *must* be a Leading Indicator that makes new business creation possible. (The total number of dials made to brand new contacts, for instance.)

4. The Specific Activities that support new business development should, when totaled up, eventually account for something like 40% of your team's total time spent at work during a typical week. When I first start

working with a sales team, however, the prospecting time investment is likely to be at about 5%.

5. Make sure you choose prospecting metrics that are relevant if your people are working on "installed accounts" only. New business is still new business, even though you may be talking about it with someone you have done dozens of deals with in the past.

6. At least one of your Specific Activities should reflect presentations or demonstrations made to "live" prospects.

7. At least one of your team's Specific Activities should reflect deals closed this week. Remember: As the manager, you should make a point of *not* overemphasizing this metric. The idea is to reward your team with favorable attention for "eating the elephant one bite a time" – not just for having finished the last bite of elephant. The closing number is there to give them a sense of continuity and cause-and-effect over an extended period of weeks.

8. Another of your team's Specific Activities should reflect the total number of brand-new opportunities the salesperson uncovered this week. As the person leading the meeting, you must help each member team to identify and recognize the opportunities within this number that represent your organization's ideal prospect profile, or "sweet spot," and thus the best bets for high-margin,

repeat business. *Everyone on your team must develop a sense of what these "sweet spot" prospects look like.*

9. If you include a metric for "servicing" current prospects or customers, make sure you probe each and every summary of this metric so that you can figure out how much time the person actually spent on "firefighting." As you might imagine, these are service requests that cannot possibly result in new business. (They typically come from your organization's lowest-margin customers.) Many of the sales teams I work with are used to spending nearly half of their total working time on this kind of firefighting. This pattern may express itself in the salesperson claiming to have "saved" the account in a way that no one else in the organization could have. Meeting by meeting, week by week, you're going to change the sales team's time investment from "saving" business that is already on the books to identifying and exploiting new selling opportunities.

10. Be open to the possibility that you will need to revise what you're measuring over time as the team's level of experience, product offerings, or selling process changes. For instance, you might have been tracking completed credit applications for the past year, but now you've decided to track followed-up quotes instead. Why? To encourage your team only to make presentations to people

who are already familiar with your service or offering and your terms and conditions.

In the next chapter, I'll share some thoughts on the most effective ways to discuss KPIs with your salespeople during the meeting.

CHAPTER
Thirteen

Specific Activities: No Questions Wrapped Around Two-by-Fours

*T*here is a great deal more to say about SPECIFIC ACTIVITIES or Key Performance Indicators. Whether directly or indirectly, much of what follows in this book is concerned with the SPECIFIC ACTIVITIES your team will make part of the working culture at your organization. This chapter, however, is the last one that will focus exclusively on SPECIFIC ACTIVITIES as discussed and evaluated by Managers during the STORM meeting itself. In this chapter, I urge you to use the SPECIFIC ACTIVITIES you choose to measure each week to build your team up ... and not to tear them down.

There are basically two kinds of questions you can ask about SPE-

CIFIC ACTIVITIES: questions among peers who respect one another and questions designed to establish control and domination. If you wish your relationships with the members of your sales team to be healthy relationships, you will use only the first category of questions during your interactions with your team. You will ask questions that are curious, respectful, and rooted in objective fact. *What happened this week in terms of individual activities? How do you feel about your activity level this week? How does it compare to last week? What are the likely outcomes of those activities, given what we know from past experience about how the activities play out?* If you use questions such as these to build bridges on the topic of SPECIFIC ACTIVITIES, you will find that your team will always go the extra mile for you in executing those activities.

That's the first kind of question you can ask. Unfortunately, there is another kind of question you can use to focus on SPECIFIC ACTIVITIES. I call this kind of question a "question wrapped around a two-by-four." These are questions that are designed, not to build bridges, but to

COMPASS POINT:
Don't ask questions like "What were you thinking coming in here with numbers like this?"

humiliate, antagonize, and alienate – and to establish you as "top dog" within the group. If you choose to open the STORM meeting by ridiculing any member of your team, by attempting to intimidate them, by attempting to embarrass them, then you will find your path a considerably rougher one. Such questions might sound like this: *What were you think-*

ing coming in here with numbers like this? What were you actually doing for all of last week? How do you think you're going to succeed here if you keep on performing at this level? Do you realize your job is on the line?

These are the questions that make constructive STORM meetings impossible. Here's why: They are merely questions wrapped around a two-by-four! They are not attempts to initiate a dialogue, but rather assaults on the salesperson – in front of his or her peers. If you choose to open your meetings with this second type of question, you will not only be wasting your time and the time of your salespeople, but also wasting a precious opportunity: the opportunity to unite your team behind someone they respect – you.

The STORM System is based on mutual respect. If you open the meeting with questions that make that respect impossible, you might as well stop measuring activity altogether.

Whenever you discuss KPIs with your people, always adopt a tone of civility, respect, and curiosity. If you have specific performance issues to discuss with a salesperson, do that in private. During the meeting, focus on the facts in front of you and only the facts in front of you. Do not pass judgment on or attack the salesperson about his or her SPECIFIC ACTIVITIES.

CHAPTER
Fourteen

The Top Five: Exercise the Pipeline

*T*he next part of the discussion in the STORM meeting will be about this salesperson's **top five** *active* prospects, as chosen by the salesperson. In this part of the meeting, each of your people should be ready, willing, and eager to discuss what has happened, is currently happening, and is about to happen with each of his or her "top five."

I mentioned that these must be "active" prospects. Technically, "active" means that the sales process for each of these five deals is clearly in process, is moving forward in some quantifiable way, includes a clear appointment of some kind between the salesperson and the decision maker, and is unfolding within a buying cycle that makes sense to you, the manager. As I say, that's the technical definition. As a practical matter, though, "active" simply means that the salesperson is willing to stake his or her credibility on the proposition that something interesting and worthy of team discussion will happen to move the deal forward over the next STORM meeting or two.

COMPASS POINT:
What are the top five active prospects?

Just as we're going to trust the salesperson to manage his or her own metrics, we're going to trust, up to a point, his or her assessment of whether an opportunity is "active." The key phrase there is "up to a point." *If the same deal stays at exactly the same status, and shows no forward motion for two straight meetings, without anything interesting happening, then you as the manager should strongly consider exercising your right to exclude it from the next "top five" list.* Ideally, that's something that the salesperson, and each member of the sales team, is going to learn to do on their own: kick inactive leads off the "top five." Until they learn to do it, however, you must be ready to do it for them.

The act of selecting five *active* prospects to discuss, each and every week, has to bring about a kind of reality check for both the individual salesperson and the team as a whole. This reality check needs to become part of your selling culture. So if someone insists on putting the same five leads up for the "top five" discussion week after week with no visible change in status on any of the prospects, that should not only attract your attention, it should also set off your team's instincts that something's wrong. Everyone else taking part in the meeting – not just you – should notice what's happening and take issue with that pattern. Why? Because it's an indication that the salesperson is not exercising his or her pipeline, which is a euphemism for "flushing the pipeline."

Flushing the pipeline is what keeps things real. It's part of the salesperson's job description. If it isn't happening, there's a problem. Your team must sense that there has to be a certain amount of predictable turnover in the "top five" each week. Some opportunities will close, while others will fall off the list. That's a fact of sales life, and someone who's committed to ignoring that fact should attract attention from the rest of the group.

Sometimes managers ask me what they should do about brand new salespeople who don't yet have five active prospects to talk about. The answer here is pretty simple: these people fall into a special category, and have a special grace period. For a period of time that corresponds to the normal "ramp-up" time you allow for new members of your team to get up and running, you will let this person include "inactive" leads on the

COMPASS POINT:

Brand new salespeople who don't yet have five active prospects to talk about fall into a special category. Allow new members to get up and running—let them have a special grace period.

"top five" list. Let things slide beyond that point and you can rest assured that you're sending the wrong message to the rest of the team.

Another common question about this portion of the STORM

meeting has to do with the various sales process management systems that sales teams use (or misuse) in tracking their activity. How do you synchronize the "top five" discussion with those systems? What do you do if you don't *have* such a system? I'll answer these questions in the next chapter.

CHAPTER
Fifteen

The Top Five: The Leader's "EDGE"

*T*he STORM System is meant to be "agnostic" when it comes to sales pipeline management systems. It can be easily adapted to any system your team is presently using. If your team is not yet using a system to manage and classify its base of business or is misusing the system that you have, you can use a tool that I developed specifically for the STORM meeting's "top five" discussion. I call it the EDGE.

COMPASS POINT:

Your tracking system should not be an encyclopedia of everything that the representative ever said to a customer, prospect, or lead.

CHAPTER FIFTEEN

The beauty of the EDGE tool lies in its simplicity. My experience is that when sales tracking and management systems don't work, it's because people try to track and do too much with them. The system should not be an encyclopedia of everything you've said to every customer, prospect, or lead over the past year. Instead, it should be a simple series of classifications that allows you to determine whether a given opportunity is active, and, if so, how far along in the sales cycle it is.

Here's the big idea: Each and every one of the opportunities your salesperson discusses during his "top five" review should fall into one of these categories:

ENGAGE: If the "top five" opportunity is in this category, it's because the salesperson is scheduled to go out on a first appointment – or, in a telemarketing environment, has had more than one good contact with the prospect. In the ENGAGE category, if you're not talking to the actual decision maker, you have to be talking to someone who can get you to the actual decision maker.

DISCOVER: If the "top five" opportunity is in this category, it's because the salesperson is engaged in the initial stages of talking to the decision maker – and also has a scheduled meeting or conversation on the calendar with that decision maker.

GIVE AND GET: If the "top five" opportunity is in this category, it's because the salesperson is *giving information to, and getting information from,* the decision maker – and has a scheduled meeting or conversation on the calendar with that decision maker.

EXECUTE: If the "top five" opportunity is in this category, it's because the decision maker is now acting and talking like a customer. The sale is statistically imminent. That doesn't mean it will come through every time, but it does mean that *most* people who make it into this category turn into customers.

Put it all together and you've got the sale's leader's EDGE!

In order to be part of the "top five" discussion, the opportunity *must* fall into one of the four categories above (or its equivalent in another tracking system). If none of the criteria above seem to apply, you, the manager, should reclassify the opportunity as STALLED. That means there's no forward motion in the opportunity and it's not active. Ask the salesperson to replace it with another "live" lead.

Sometimes members of the sales team disagree with us about whether an opportunity really deserves to be STALLED. The acid test here is very simple: Is the prospect returning calls or emails? If the salesperson has something in the top five, but has no record of return calls or e-mail messages, then it's actually STALLED and does not belong in the "top five."

The beauty of the EDGE system – or any effective prospect tracking system – is that it rewards people for "hitting singles." By allowing the members of your team to talk about incremental progress on their five most promising opportunities, you take the pressure off your people, make it easier for them to share best practices that they've discovered along the way, and powerfully motivate them to move one or more of the opportunities forward for next week's discussion.

CHAPTER
Sixteen

Others Who Can Help and Resources Needed

The next two boxes are simple but powerful tools for turning the meeting into a dialogue rather than a monologue. I'm covering them both in a single chapter because they both serve the same purpose: *giving salespeople an opportunity to talk in public about the help they need.* Psychologically, this is a vitally important component; if you skip it by short changing either box, your meetings will not succeed. It's as simple as that.

When you ask your people to discuss the "Others Who Can Help" box, you give them a chance to tell you, and the team as a whole, exactly who they think could help them move one or more deals forward.

CHAPTER SIXTEEN

These deals may connect to the top five they've been discussing or may be entirely different. The point is, if the salesperson needs someone to offer insights, advice, experience, referrals, or even in-person assistance with an upcoming meeting, they can ask for it here. Many of your salespeople will make a habit of operating under the assumption that they never need anyone's help to close any sale. This box isn't exactly an instant remedy for that tendency, which goes back to the whole "magical selling" problem, but it is a weekly reminder that help is available for the asking. It's also a chance to compliment and stroke other members of the team, which may produce more team cohesion and more of a feeling of being an "ensemble."

Discussions about the next box, "Resources Needed," offer the salesperson the chance to ask, not for the assistance of specific people, but for *stuff*: new brochures, product samples, training, books, audiotapes, or access to other internal resources and professional development tools. This box also gives each member of your team – let's face it – the opportunity to complain a little bit about something they need and aren't getting. That's fine. It's better for them to complain publicly for three minutes than for them to spend a day and a half complaining about it behind your back.

If you don't let the members of your sales team use the STORM meeting to talk in detail about exactly what they need in the areas of people or stuff, one of two bad things will happen. The first bad thing is that they'll assume they never get what they want and build up lingering resentments about that problem. And the second bad thing is that they'll start trying to do everything – including things they shouldn't be doing – entirely on their own. That's what makes sales cycles lengthen and sales productivity drop.

Just a little effort from your side will keep the conversation focused, and keep things from degenerating into a "pity party." You may be tempted to skip over these two boxes or to ask your people to e-mail you about what they need instead of "taking up time in the meeting" with these subjects. Fight that temptation! It takes only a few minutes to let the members of your team each say exactly what they need to say about the people and resources they need. Let them!

COMPASS POINT:
It's your job to keep the conversation focused.

CHAPTER
Seventeen

The STORM Plan:
MOVEMENT PROJECTED

*E*ach member of your team must be prepared, week in and week out, to discuss the MOVEMENT PROJECTED on a specific deal in the coming week – and also review whether or not the MOVEMENT PROJECTED last week actually occurred.

Your salesperson's final job as his or her "turn" concludes is to make an intelligent, reality-based *prediction* about a prospect that has already moved forward in some measurable way in your organization's sales process. Your team member should say clearly what he or she thinks will have happened with a given prospect by the time the next meeting rolls around. No, the salesperson can't simply say, "I plan to call ABC

Company and ask for an appointment" – because that's not a prediction of *prospect* behavior. Instead, the salesperson could say, "I project that I will set my first meeting with the President of ABC Company by this time next week."

Being able to anticipate, and discuss, prospect behavior that the salesperson thinks will have taken place "one week from today" is a critical part of the STORM System. In fact, this is one of the major cultural changes that takes place, on both the group and the individual level, as a result of implementing STORM. No, the salesperson's not always going to be "on target" when the next meeting takes place, but the salesperson *is* going to have an opportunity to explain what happened (or didn't happen) and why – and make another prediction for next week.

COMPASS POINT:
*Debrief – tactfully – on "what we thought was going to happen,"
what actually happened, and "what we're going to do next."*

As a practical matter, when you reach this point in the meeting, you will tactfully "debrief" with the salesperson on "what we thought was going to happen," what actually did happen, and "what we're going to do next." The discussion should always be about the actions the salesperson took, the specific result the salesperson anticipated, or the actions the salesperson wants to pursue next. The prospect that your salesperson predicts movement on this week does not have to be the same one he or she predicted movement on last week.

If for some reason the salesperson has no actual forward movement to report on any front, with any prospect, at any point during the STORM meeting, you will need to acknowledge that fact openly before the group, without apology. Do this in a way that lets all the other team members know, without intimidation or name-calling, that this is a problem. There really is "no place to hide" when it comes to starting the STORM meeting.

COMPASS POINT:

There should be "no place to hide" when it comes to discussions of forward movement in the sales process. Either there was movement in a given opportunity this week, or there wasn't.

Below, you'll find some examples of outcomes that constitute "movement" during this part of the meeting and also examples of topics where you should push back and (politely) insist on something more tangible from your salesperson during the discussion.

MOVEMENT IS ....

"I got the signed contract in for the deal with ABC Company."

"I scheduled a face-to-face meeting with Joe Smith, Executive Vice President. It's taking place Monday at 3:00 pm in his office."

"I scheduled a conference call with five key people about what should go into our proposal. It's going to happen next Tuesday at 4:00 pm."

"I met for the first time with Sharon Cutlass and she agreed to meet with me again next week."

"Based on input from a variety of key people including the CEO, I made a presentation to the executive committee. They have promised me a decision on Monday morning."

"I got a meeting with the CEO to review our performance as a major vendor and set up a plan for the next year."

MOVEMENT IS *NOT*:

"ABC Company told me they are looking at the contract."

"I left a message with Joe Smith, Executive Vice President."

"They want to schedule a teleconference and are going to let me know when it can happen."

"I met for the first time with Sharon Cutlass. She asked me to call back next week sometime to set up a new appointment after things calm down in the office."

"I was all set to make a presentation before the executive committee,

but I couldn't because (insert long, drawn-out story here). I'm going to call them back on Monday and try again."

"I had a very good discussion with the CEO's executive assistant. She said she thought she would be able to set up a meeting sometime next week."

CHAPTER
Eighteen

Preparing for the "Real" STORM Meeting

t's likely that your very first STORM meeting will simply set the stage for the five elements you've just learned about – and set your team on notice that, starting next week, they will in fact be filling out the STORM sheet each and every week, no matter what, prior to their participation in this weekly discussion. During the initial meeting, you'll also want to emphasize the point that the STORM sheet should take no longer than 45 minutes to prepare.

> **COMPASS POINT:**
> *Use e-mail messages to help the team prepare for the meeting.*

You'll be laying the groundwork for an informal, but extremely important part of the "real" STORM meeting – the time tracking discussion. Although they won't have to fill out any part of the STORM sheet with time information, they should be ready to discuss, and send you an e-mail before the meeting with *rough* estimates of the following:

* How much *time* they spent in the previous week on each of the Key Performance Indicators.

* How much *time* they spent servicing accounts.

* How much *time* of that servicing total was spent on "firefighting" activities.

There's a very simple way to track this information and you'll want to set it up during this first, "preparatory" STORM meeting – the one that comes before the "real" STORM meeting with "real" numbers. Each of your team members should get used to noting, briefly, what they're doing in half-hour increments during the working day, either by filling in the details in a personal notebook or by making very brief entries in their calendar system, such as Outlook or Yahoo! Calendar.

Important: I'm not talking about filling out and passing in "time sheets." I'm talking about making an *informal, rough estimate*

COMPASS POINT:

The mini-STORM planner's design helps your team members keep track of their time.

of how the sixteen half-hour segments in a typical working day were actually spent and then being ready to discuss those estimates at the end of the week during the next STORM meeting.

I like to encourage members of the sales team to carry around a little mini-STORM planner, especially designed with nine slots in it for carrying nine or ten blank three by five cards. On the first five cards, the team should have the name and contact information for the Top Five they've just identified during your "initial" storm meeting. On the remaining four or five cards, they can put a tic-mark down each time they spend the majority of any thirty-minute segment of the day on each of the KPIs. They should also use a card to record how much time they spend "firefighting."

This little book fits in the shirt or coat pocket, and is an excellent reinforcement for the STORM System in between meetings. It takes no more "discipline" or "paperwork" to make entries in this little book than it takes to keep track of calories consumed, laps swum, or any other meaningful indicator we choose to track in our lives. The numbers on the mini-STORM Planner don't have to be 100% accurate, but they should be *roughly* accurate – accurate enough to summarize beforehand for the manager and discuss during the meeting!

This little notebook, which I would recommend but not insist that you pass out at your first "preliminary" meeting, is a silent reminder of the STORM process. All week long, it asks:

* Are you going to get around to taking action on your Top Five – or not?

* Are you going to track your time – or not?

* Are you going to be ready for the meeting next week – or not?

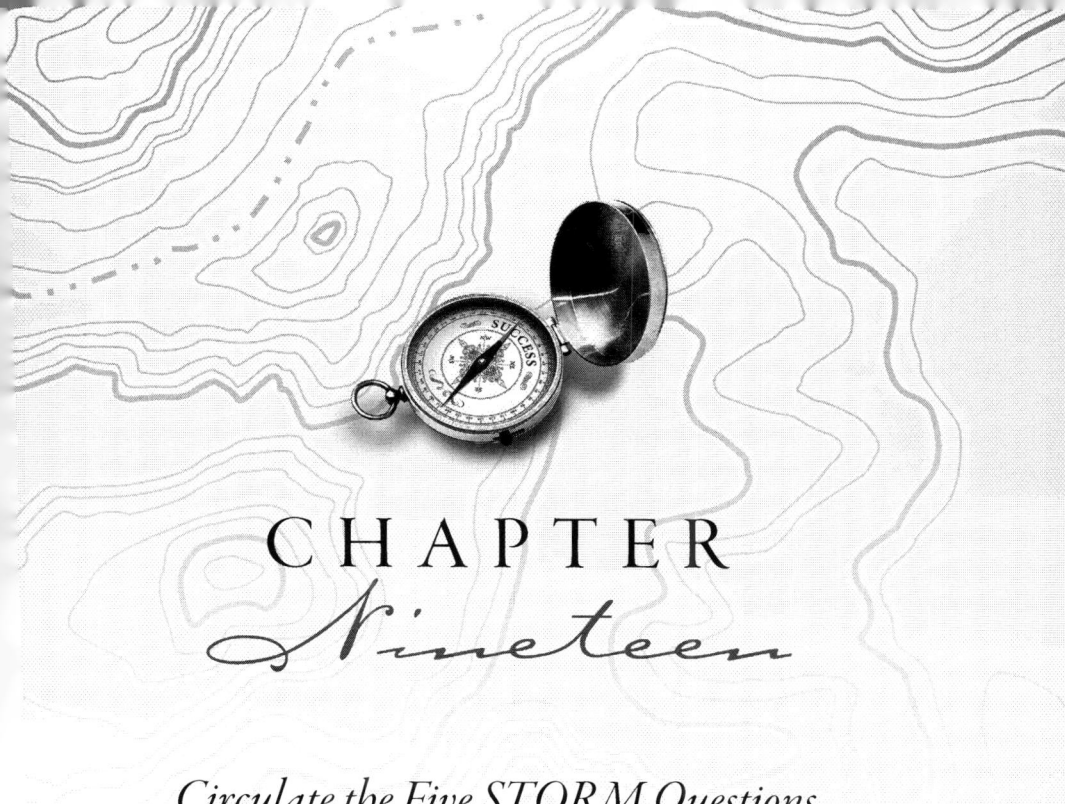

CHAPTER
Nineteen

Circulate the Five STORM Questions

O nce you've set the stage for the "real" STORM meeting, your team should start preparing to answer five very specific questions about their planning, presentation, and selling activities. You must help them prepare! In addition to passing out the blank STORM plan sheets, you should also adapt, circulate, and discuss the following list of questions which will help the team to complete the STORM PLAN for the first time. These questions will serve as a resource for future meetings as well.

Remind the team repeatedly that they really will be responsible for responding to each question on the list during the next STORM meeting. Remind them that they must forward a copy of the completed STORM PLAN to you at least 24 hours before the next STORM meeting begins!

COMPASS POINT:

Each member of the team must forward a copy of the completed STORM PLAN to you at least 24 hours before the next STORM meeting begins.

QUESTION ONE: WHAT WERE MY SPECIFIC ACTIVITIES THIS WEEK? (for instance:)

TOTAL DIALS (where "dial" means picking up the phone to call an individual in an attempt to generate revenue, and can only apply to one person called during a single 24-hour period).

TOTAL CONVERSATIONS (where "conversation" means a voice-to-voice discussion with a decision maker or someone we believe to be a decision maker).

TOTAL FACE-TO-FACE MEETINGS (where "face-to-face meeting" means a physical appointment with a decision maker that has actually taken place).

TOTAL SALES: (where "sales" means "closed deals").

QUESTION TWO: WHAT ARE MY TOP FIVE SELLING OPPORTUNITIES? (These must be active prospects unless the salesperson has no active prospects.)

QUESTION THREE: WHO ARE THE OTHERS WHO CAN HELP ME IN THE WEEK FOLLOWING THE NEXT STORM MEETING? (THESE ARE PEOPLE WHO CAN HELP MOVE ONE OR MORE SALES FORWARD.)

QUESTION FOUR: WHAT ARE THE RESOURCES THAT WILL HELP ME IN THE WEEK FOLLOWING THE NEXT STORM MEETING? (This is a request for "stuff" that can help move one or more opportunities forward.)

QUESTION FIVE: WHAT MOVEMENT DO I PROJECT IN THE WEEK FOLLOWING THE NEXT STORM MEETING? (This movement forward must connect to a specific selling opportunity. It can connect to the EDGE tracking system I've shared with you in this book or with any other sales tracking system you have in place.)

The more time you spend reviewing these questions ahead of time, the better prepared your team will be for the STORM meeting. Print, hand out, and e-mail the questions and their explanation to everyone in addition to giving them the blank STORM plan to fill out.

If a member of your team does not forward the answers to these questions to you *before* the STORM meeting and is not prepared to answer them verbally *during* the meeting, that team member is not prepared for the meeting!

CHAPTER
Twenty

The Manager's Feedback Form

We come now to one of the most important elements of the STORM System: the Manager's Feedback Form. You will complete this form *before* the meeting – and share it immediately *afterwards*.

> **COMPASS POINT:**
> *If there's no feedback from you, there's going to be no positive change.*

The Feedback Form is absolutely essential; don't skip it. If you want to drive positive change, you've got to be able to provide consistent feedback. If there's no feedback, there's going to be no positive change. What's more, if there's the wrong *kind* of feedback, there's going to be no positive change. The Manager's Feedback Form helps you give the right kind of feedback in a format that your team can benefit from both collectively and as individuals.

The Feedback Form has two variations: one for the whole team, which everyone sees and one for the individual salesperson, which only the manager and the individual salesperson see, during a private meeting. In each variation, this simple rule applies: *focus on the behaviors, not on the outcomes.* Don't get worked up about whether a given deal has closed, whether the right number of sales has closed, or whether a particular salesperson is making the right impression on you. Focus, each and every week, on the behaviors that *drive* sales – not on the people who *make* sales.

Figure 20.1 is an example of a completed Manager's Feedback Form for the team as a whole. You might summarize this briefly at the conclusion of the meeting – and share the complete form with the whole team (perhaps via e-mail) right *after* the STORM meeting.

The team form serves a dual purpose: it not only summarizes your feedback for the team, but it also serves as a great "thumbnail sketch" for your own boss – or anyone else in top management – about exactly how the team is performing: What's working in terms of daily and weekly activity, what still needs improvement, and your best input on what the team should be focusing on in the coming week.

Figure 20.2 is an an example of what a personalized Manager's Feedback Form would look like for an individual salesperson. Again, this is meant to be reviewed by two and only two people: The salesperson and his or her manager.

FIGURE 20.1: Manager's Feedback Form for the entire team

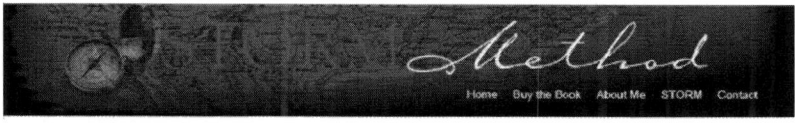

ADMINISTRATOR PANEL

Print

STORM REPORT
07/06/2009 - 07/13/2009

Overall Progress:

Category	Score	Goal	Difference
% Time Servicing	30	20	10
% Time Selling Existing	3	30	- 27
% Time Firefighting	3	10	- 7
% Time Prospecting	63	35	28

CATEGORY

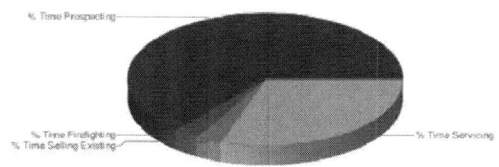

This Week's #1 Opportunity	
Name	Notes
Lively, Josh	AM Express Happy AM Express Yogi
Newcomb, Jim	Montgomery's Mkt
Pruitt, Tim	BUTCHER SHOP

This Week's #1 Success	
Name	Notes
Lively, Josh	Yogi Happy
Newcomb, Jim	New Center Market
Pruitt, Tim	FENTRESS CO-OP

Others Who Can Help	
Name	Notes
Lively, Josh	n/a
Newcomb, Jim	n/a
Pruitt, Tim	NA

Resources Needed	
Name	Notes
Lively, Josh	Pricing Customers Daily
Newcomb, Jim	n/a
Pruitt, Tim	NA

91

FIGURE 20.2: Manager's Feedback Form for an individual salesperson.

Lively, Josh		Good
% Time Servicing Score: Excellent Value: 1	**User Notes:**	**Evaluation Notes:** Josh keep up the good work
% Time Selling Existing Score: Needs Improvement Value: 0	**User Notes:**	**Evaluation Notes:** Josh no worries you are just starting out
% Time Firefighting Score: Excellent Value: 0	**User Notes:**	**Evaluation Notes:** Continue to stay focused
% Time Prospecting Score: Excellent Value: 99	**User Notes:**	**Evaluation Notes:** Prospecting will continue to grow the business
New Customers Value: 0	**User Notes:**	**Evaluation Notes:** Your pipeline is strong

Pruitt, Tim		Needs Improvement
% Time Servicing Score: Needs Improvement Value: 40	**User Notes:**	**Evaluation Notes:** Tim way too much time here
% Time Selling Existing Score: Needs Improvement Value: 0	**User Notes:**	**Evaluation Notes:** You need to upsell account planning can help
% Time Firefighting Score: Excellent Value: 0	**User Notes:**	**Evaluation Notes:** This is good news

This document should be the topic of a brief one-on-one meeting (either face-to-face or voice-to-voice) between the sales manager and the salesperson to plan the week to come. That meeting should take no more than ten or fifteen minutes and it should take place *each and every week, without exception.* That's because you don't want the members of your team getting used to the pattern of only getting "called into the office" when there's a problem! If the salesperson just had a great week in terms of the metrics you're measuring, have a brief meeting to share your feedback as recorded on the Feedback Form. If the salesperson had a terrible week, have a brief meeting to share your feedback, too.

Whether you're delivering the "team as a whole" message or the "just between you and me" message, be sure to follow these guidelines when giving feedback.

* *Don't* comment on individual deals that did or didn't close. I know I've said this before, but it's so important that I'm repeating it twice in the same chapter. Focus *exclusively* on measurable Key Performance Indicators – both leading and lagging indicators.

* *Don't* comment on any prospect that appears in anyone's Top Five.

* *Don't* second-guess the prospects your salespeople have chosen to work on. If they think it's important, it's important.

* *Do* make the Feedback Form clear and understandable.

* *Do* classify weekly performance against particular KPIs as Excellent, Acceptable, and Unacceptable. If you can, color-code your feedback form so that Excellent performance is rendered in green, Acceptable performance is rendered in yellow, and Unacceptable performance is rendered against a red background. You don't have to explain what green, yellow, and red mean: they'll get the message.

* *Do* complete the Feedback Form on a timely basis, week after week.

* *Do* link all of your comments to Mutually Agreed Upon Objectives.

CHAPTER
Twenty-One

The Moment of Truth

mmediately upon completing your first honest-to-good-ness STORM meeting, you, the manager, will face what I call a MOMENT OF TRUTH. This moment is fateful because it's at precisely this point that managers make one of four classic, and potentially disastrous, mistakes. I've outlined them below.

COMPASS POINT:

*Avoid the four classic mistakes managers make
when implementing the STORM System.*

CHAPTER TWENTY-ONE

CLASSIC MISTAKE NUMBER ONE: Micromanaging. Some managers run a good STORM meeting as I've outlined it in this book, but then start trying to micromanage things *after* the meeting – things that they know they're not supposed to try to micromanage *during* the meeting. If you're going to change the culture in your sales team, you must prove to them that you are willing to manage according to the philosophy, principles, and standards you have set for yourself, and for them, during the STORM session. Specifically, this means letting the individual members of your team have full responsibility and accountability for managing the Top Five prospects they've just identified. If they ask you for help, give it to them. If you have *brief, respectful* suggestions to pass along – suggestions that leave the members of your team in charge of what happens next – that's fine. But don't start "grilling" people after the meeting. Give them ownership of the process. If something is in the Top Five, it's either going to close or fall off the list of active prospects in the short term. If you have a big problem with something the rep is doing, incorporate it briefly as part of your *individual* feedback. Ask: "What happened?" Then wait for the answer. Yes, this takes discipline. But that's why they made you a manager, right?

CLASSIC MISTAKE NUMBER TWO: Not scheduling the next meeting *immediately* after concluding this meeting. If you and your people don't put the next meeting on the calendar, you're not doing your job as a manager. *If the STORM meeting is not a regular, predictable part of your team's calendar, the STORM System will not work.* As you begin the process, schedule the meetings for once a week – and make sure you follow through on the schedule. Do not skip meetings!

CLASSIC MISTAKE NUMBER THREE: Not reminding the

members of your team that they must forward their STORM reports to you at least 24 hours before the next STORM meeting. This is something they must get into the habit of doing. It is a non-negotiable requirement for anyone who wishes to work on your team. Do not let *any* member of your team neglect this brief planning and review exercise! If necessary, sit down with the salesperson and complete the form with him or her until it becomes second nature.

CLASSIC MISTAKE NUMBER FOUR: Not preparing your own Feedback Forms based on the STORM reports you receive from the team. These, too, must be as regular as clockwork. If you are not willing to model the same consistency you expect from the team, the STORM System will not work for you.

Avoid these four errors (and, let's face it, they are fairly easy to avoid) and you will find that your team "ramps up" to the system with relative ease.

CHAPTER
Twenty-Two

No Excuses!

*Y*ou've now seen the basics of the system. I'm hoping you're excited by it. I certainly am!

As enthusiastic as I am about STORM, I realize that it probably represents a major change in the way you're now doing things with your team. You've got questions, I'm sure, and it's possible you've even got some misgivings about making this a regular feature of your team's selling routine. In the chapters that follow, I'll try to answer the most common questions about running effective STORM meetings. In this chapter, I'll try to overcome some of the most common obstacles people cite for either not implementing the system at all or (just as bad) implementing it inconsistently!

As you'll see, I take a NO EXCUSES approach when it comes to implementing the STORM System ... the same approach I hope you'll take when you implement it with your team.

COMPASS POINT:

Don't accept excuses for not following the STORM System.
Don't make excuses, either.

The metrics you've been using in previous chapters aren't right for my team. So pick different things to measure! The beauty of the system is that it's completely flexible. You can change the metrics over time as the need arises, and you certainly don't have to use the metrics I've suggested. Use the metrics to fix specific issues that arise on your team!

I don't have time for this. Let me be frank. If you can't make time to do this weekly meeting – and once you get the hang of it, you'll be talking about investing a few hours a week to get ready for the STORM meeting and an hour a week to conduct it – you're in the wrong line of work.

I hate paperwork. Make a commitment to do it anyway for a couple of hours a week. You'll make your own planning easier, *and* support your team as it learns to get better at planning. Without planning, your team is doomed to under-perform –and you'll be doomed to issuing quarterly "disaster reports" (which is still paperwork, just far more painful paperwork). Wouldn't you rather give your team, and your own superiors, a window on what's actually happening each week? Wouldn't you rather give them meaningful feedback about what's working and what isn't?

Don't think of any of this as paperwork. Think of it as the tools you use to change behavior and transform the "department" into a business in its own right.

We're already doing fine without this. Are you sure? Is your revenue growing, despite whatever is happening in the larger economy? Are your own revenue projections accurate? Are you sure your team will exceed quota? If they didn't, who would be held responsible? Is your own job safe in both the short and long term? Are *any* members of your team in danger of "plateau-ing?" Do you know for sure what the team's best practices are? Could you summarize them for a new salesperson, or for your company's top managers? Are you effectively reinforcing what *each* team member is already doing well? Are you identifying and correcting weaknesses, both on the personal and the team level? Are you coaching your people to maximize those strengths and overcome those weaknesses, on a one-on-one basis, once a week? Do those coaching sessions support your employee evaluation and retention program? **If your answer to any of these questions was "No" (or even, "I'm not sure,") you're definitely *not* doing fine without this!**

It's just not my style. I'm more of an intuitive manager. You can still be intuitive using the STORM System. In fact, you can be even *more* intuitive because you'll have evidence to back up your intuition. You'll be able to prove to higher-ups that your "gut instinct" is on target!

Here's the bottom line. Companies who are doing this are now growing their businesses – while their competitors who *aren't* doing this are struggling. Why are they struggling? Because they're not using a critical resource – their own sales team – efficiently. Make no mistake. Your organization's salespeople really are an expensive resource. The system

I've shared with you, and am about to troubleshoot for you, represents the best available tool for protecting that resource!

Give your people an hour a week – prepare for that hour – and keep at it, week after week. You won't regret your decision to protect your team, your organization, and yourself – with the STORM System!

CHAPTER
Twenty-Three

What's The Easiest Way To Screw This Up?

’m tackling this question first because its answer is the most important of all, as well as the simplest. The easiest way to screw the STORM system up is *not to hold the meetings on a weekly basis.*

The first six weeks are particularly critical here in terms of getting the system up and running, and setting people's expectations about what is really going to happen, week after week. But even after those first few weeks pass, and the initial awkwardness fades, the message must get through to each and every member of your team: Preparing for the meeting, and taking part in it, is part of working here. No ifs, ands, or buts.

Every week your salespeople come to work must pose the question: *Are you ready for the meeting?* With weekly meetings, we are telling our people that it's important that they create a weekly plan for themselves. Without weekly meetings, we are telling them that it doesn't matter whether they have a weekly plan for themselves. It's that simple.

COMPASS POINT:

With weekly meetings, we are telling our people that it's important that they create a weekly plan for themselves.

You can customize the weekly meetings into whatever routine works best for you. My own experience is that conference calls are a particularly effective format. Even if somebody's off-site, or traveling to meet with a major account, or working from home that day, the team gets to gather "virtually" for the meeting by phone. That may or may not be your favorite meeting format ... but *some* consistent format needs to emerge as the reason each member of the team prepares that weekly plan.

If the meetings are sporadic, they won't work. You and everyone else will be wasting time participating in them.

If, on the other hand, they are a 52-weeks-a-year, no-kidding, where-the-hell-were you reality of selling for your organization, these meetings will transform your organization's culture.

The STORM meeting *must* become a company ritual. Everyone *must* understand and buy into the format. It's your job to make sure that they do, no matter how unfamiliar the meetings may feel at first. **Be persistent.**

Nothing in the world can take the place of Persistence. Talent will not; nothing is more common than unsuccessful men with talent. Genius will not; unrewarded genius is almost a proverb. Education will not; the world is full of educated derelicts. Persistence and determination alone are omnipotent. The slogan 'Press On' has solved and always will solve the problems of the human race.

−CALVIN COOLIDGE

CHAPTER
Twenty-Four

What if They Show Up,
but Don't Complete the STORM Plan?

Hey, it happens. Just make sure you respond appropriately the very *first* time it happens.

Don't overreact. Point out that the STORM plan is a required element for the meeting, and ask the salesperson to make sure he or she prepares it for the next meeting. Mention that during the meeting, then send a *short* e-mail immediately after the meeting where the person showed up without his or her STORM plan. The e-mail should say, more or less, "Please make sure you have your STORM plan ready for the next meeting." Send a similar *short* e-mail about 48 hours before the next meeting. If the person shows up *again* without the paperwork, remind him or her that the STORM plan is mandatory, listen briefly to the "summary from memory," then move on to the next person. Don't give the non-complier any additional energy during the meeting; just keep moving.

COMPASS POINT:
Just keep moving.

Don't make a Federal case out of this. Don't get emotional. Don't fuel a conflict. Just keep pushing and keep reiterating the standard. In the vast majority of cases, your simple, low-key reminders will be enough.

There are three types of people who are going to be coming to this meeting: true believers, who will trust your instincts and write down everything you say during the meeting; people who like what they hear, but aren't quite sure whether or not they should buy into STORM; and the "runners and gunners," the top performers who have seen everything and done everything and may take a little convincing to pick up this system and run with it.

Here's the strategy. You've already got the first group, so all you have to do is praise them and thank them for participating. The third group isn't going to do anything it doesn't want to do, and you can't fire them, so consider getting them to show up for the meetings to be a victory, at least for the first few weeks. Your goal should be to get the people *in the middle,* that second group, to sign on to the system and start working it week after week. If necessary, have private meetings with the "on the fence" folks in the second group and help them to fill out their STORM plans ahead of time.

Once the "runners and gunners" realize that a) everyone else is using the system and b) they're missing out on a chance to show off how brilliant they are and how many best practices they've mastered – they'll come around.

If possible, get the CEO, founder, or owner of the company to sit in on the meetings for the first six weeks. This will help you with compliance during this critical period.

CHAPTER
Twenty-Five

How Long Until We Start to See Results?

*T*his is a very common question. In practice, the answer is as simple or as complex as you choose to make it.

If you follow the system as I've laid it out, and *if* you are sure to involve senior management in the first two or three meetings, and *if* you follow through to make the meetings a consistent, weekly part of the company culture, then you'll probably start to see measurable positive results within 45 to 90 days. That's the simple answer.

Most teams I work with don't have any problem meeting all three of those conditions, and as a result, it typically doesn't take them all that long to get to the point where their people start to bring new business to the table. Some teams, though, find reasons not to execute on those three *ifs*. As a result, they complicate matters and have a longer learning curve.

I've already emphasized the importance of following the program as you've seen it explained here -- and the necessity of holding the meetings, no matter what. It's worth looking closely at the role that "buy-in" from people at the top will have in accelerating your team's performance under the STORM System.

Some sales managers are hesitant to bring senior people in on the initial STORM meetings -- because they're afraid that they'll be held to an unrealistic time or performance standard by those senior officers. Actually, senior management is your best ally in implementing a system like this. The top people are unlikely to expect instant or quota-shattering performance from you; they know that they can't expect good things to happen in a few days or weeks. They want to see a change in the way the sales team is operating even more than you do.

Take the initiative. Ask the highest-ranking person you can find to sit in on the initial meetings and perhaps even give an opening message that translates as "Yes, you really are expected to do this." Once you do that, you'll make it absolutely clear that all team members have no excuse not to take part ... and you'll reduce the time gap between implementation and improved commissions.

Even if the program takes, say, six months to deliver measurable,

COMPASS POINT:
*Bring your organization's senior people in
on the initial STORM meetings.*

sustainable changes in culture and income – and that's at the outer edge of the curve – that's not all that long a time span for the kinds of changes we're talking about. Presidents, owners, and C-level executives are willing to give the program the time it needs to take root. In the meantime, planning is taking place, key indicators are being measured and discussed, the working environment has become more professional, and best practices are being shared. That's usually a step ahead of where the sales team was before.

So: Ask your organization's top people to participate. Let them read this book. Encourage them to take part in the initial meetings, and any meetings after that they choose to "drop in on." They'll get a snapshot of the team's performance, they'll engage with the team, they'll help you to win over skeptics, and they'll shorten your "time to results."

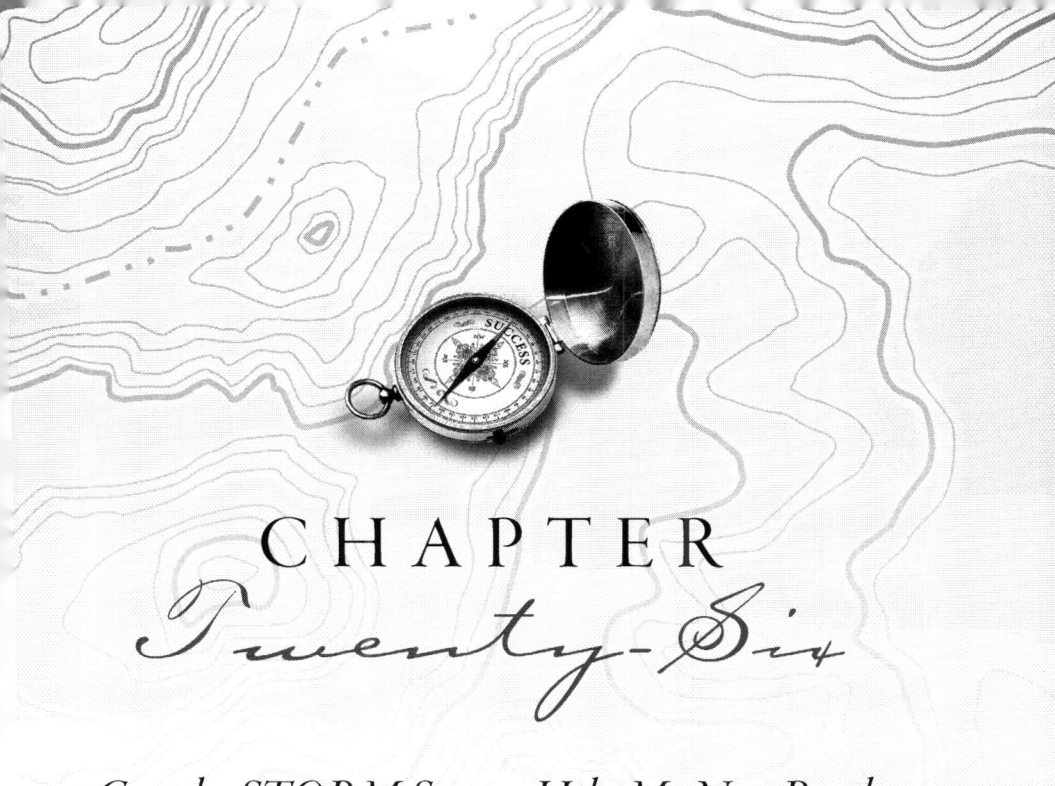

CHAPTER
Twenty-Six

Can the STORM System Help My New People Ramp Up More Quickly?

*I*t certainly can. In fact, the sooner you make this system part of your "new hire" orientation and training, the better off your entire organization will be.

That's because the first time you put a "rookie" through this process – and the first time your "rookie" begins practicing this tracking system and no other on a daily and weekly basis – the easier it will be for other members of your team to step up and help the newcomer get up and running with "the way we do things here." Once that conversation happens, the STORM System is basically locked in!

I've seen new hires in very tough industries ramp up much more quickly than their counterparts at other companies who aren't using the STORM System. The reason it works so well, of course, is that it tends to reinforce the right KPIs – and quickly move people away from lagging indicators that would otherwise slow down their "initiation period." STORM makes it easier for new salespeople to get up and running quickly, which is one of the reasons that senior executives tend to fall in love with it. Once you make it part of your orientation program, the training and recruiting investment you make in new hires tends to pay off much more quickly.

New hires who haven't had a lot of sales experience tend to be among the most faithful fans of the STORM System. That's because they haven't yet learned to be cynical about selling. They're also the most eager to learn about best practices. They're usually the quickest to see positive results from following the system. After just a few weeks, they get used to planning, executing, and contributing at the meetings ... and they also get "addicted" to learning from the senior people who offer their own insights and experience.

COMPASS POINT:

Remember that new hires who haven't had a lot of sales experience tend to be among the most faithful fans of the STORM System.

Act quickly. If you hire a new salesperson and *do not* take a day or two to introduce that person to the STORM System within the first week of coming on, you run the risk of sending the wrong signal to your current staff. The message should be clear and unequivocal – **every new person we bring on will be blocking, tackling, and practicing week in and week out, according to this system.** *Even if the person has no active sales leads to discuss,* the new hire must take part in the weekly STORM calls. (See Chapter 14 for advice on how to handle meetings with people who do not yet have sufficient activity to accumulate a Top Five.)

CHAPTER
Twenty-Seven

Can the STORM System Make It Easier for Me to Identify – and Get Rid of – Under-performers?

$\mathcal{D}$efinitely – but please understand: the very best way to "get rid" of under-performers is to give them the tools they need to hit quota, so they're no longer under-performers! The STORM System does that.

News flash: Most salespeople on your team already know who's pulling their weight and who's not. Up to this point, however, the challenge has been that that there's never been a good forum for discussing the *activities* – not the people – that have made this imbalance on your team possible. By focusing on the activities on a weekly basis, you've got a great tool for bringing problem *performance patterns* to light. Once you have a platform for identifying and publicly discussing problem *performance patterns,* your problem performers have nowhere to hide. They also have a clear choice: Start implementing different activity patterns and using the best practices everyone else is using ... or find somewhere else to work.

Given that choice, persistent under-performers who take part in STORM meetings tend to either improve or self-select and leave the team. Those are two options you can live with, right?

If someone is striking out every time, week after week after week, it quickly becomes apparent that something has to change. More often than you might imagine, the "something" that has to change is the way the underperforming team member tackles the day. Once you change the behaviors, you change the performance.

Think of the weekly STORM meeting as a big rudder and any individual person on your sales team as a boat. You're guiding, guiding, guiding – and the person is either on course, or he's not. When everyone knows that there's a problem with the person who's not on course, you're

COMPASS POINT:

*If you use the STORM System properly, problem performers
are more likely to come to you for help or to ask you what
has to happen to make the results change.*

less likely to have those "Here's what you have to do if you want to keep on working here." meetings. Do you know why? It's because the problem performer is more likely to come to you for help or to ask you what has to happen to make the results change.

If the results *don't* change, you're more likely, using the STORM System, to get a voluntary resignation than a prolonged battle about who should be on probation and who shouldn't. Nobody likes striking out ten or twelve weeks in a row. If it really isn't working, your team member will recognize that fact like everyone else. The process of moving on happens more quickly, and less traumatically, when everyone knows you've got twelve weeks of "flashing red" individual performance reports on file for this person.

CHAPTER
Twenty-Eight

The Culture of Planning

ost of the new things you try to get your team to do have a very short shelf life. Your team tries whatever you have in mind for a couple of weeks (if you're lucky), but sooner or later they get bored and want to move on to something else. Then you try to get them to keep doing the thing they're already bored with that you want them to do and they pretend to do it, in order to placate you. When you're not watching, they don't do it. Let's be realistic – that's what happens. The longer you try to do something with your team, the less effective it becomes.

CHAPTER TWENTY-EIGHT

THE STORM SYSTEM IS DIFFERENT.

In fact, the dynamics with the STORM System are just the opposite. The system you've learned in these pages works just as effectively as time goes on and usually *improves* in effectiveness as time passes. There's a reason for this. The longer you do it, the more it helps your team, and each individual within it, implement what I call a Culture of Planning. Once the STORM System has become part of the routine and has made the Culture of Planning a reality in the daily operating processes of your team, your people don't dread the meetings or buy out of them. They show up. They contribute. Even if they are senior players who are achieving at a high level and don't really "need" to hear other people's best practices, they take part in the meetings to share their own best practices, and to reinforce their own sense of being important members of the team. Why? Because the Culture of Planning, once it takes root, reinforces itself.

People learn to take part in these meetings and even start looking forward to them because the meetings have become part of *how they attain the goals that are important to them as people.* Once you make the STORM System part of the team's identity, you make the act of *planning,* on both the individual and group levels, part of the team's culture.

There's something about writing your goals down, sharing your goals with the rest of the team, and taking action on them that solidifies the goal, the plan. And I think one of the big reasons the STORM System has been so successful over the years is that it gives people an accessible, painless, user-friendly way to satisfy two very powerful human needs: the need to connect with others and the need to plan for and take action on an important goal. Because the STORM System addresses both of those basic human needs, it works.

And people don't walk away from what works.

COMPASS POINT:

Use the STORM System to satisfy two powerful human instincts: connecting with others and taking action on important goals.

Follow what I've laid out for you in the previous chapters, exactly as I've laid it out for you, and it will work because it will create a Culture of Planning within your sales team.

EPILOGUE

*T*here are a couple of things I tell people when I first lay out the STORM program for them in person.

First and foremost (and I am repeating this only because it's the most important point in the book, and warrants repetition): *Come hell or high water, the STORM meetings must happen.*

Second, I recommend, that you conduct these weekly meetings by teleconference. This increases buy-in and gives people fewer excuses not to participate during those critical early meetings. It doesn't matter whether or not people are out of the office – they can still be on the call.

Third, your company's top management doesn't need to participate in each and every meeting, *but* they do need to be invested in the fact that the process will continue. Use the system to generate weekly snapshots for them about what activity is taking place on the ground and you'll find that your senior people will give you the continued support you need to implement the program.

Fourth, remember that you, the manager, are the master of ceremonies, not the punisher. In fact, you're better off giving someone else the chance to run the call every few weeks. The meetings are not about you or your preferences as a manager; they're about a specific methodology that works regardless of who's running the meeting. After a few weeks, anyone who participates in a STORM meeting should be able to run the meeting. Take advantage of that fact.

Fifth and finally, remember to keep it simple. The weekly activity discussion is the key point; if you keep coming back to that point, you and your team will be fine. Don't get distracted by personalities, wins, losses, or anything else. Keep coming back to those simple metrics. **Keep coming back to the KPIs you're using to measure the sales people, week after week, and to the targets that the sales team is willing to set for themselves and then execute on.** From a sales management perspective, I haven't found any system that's perfect, but I have found that it's always better to stick with something that's simple and effective rather than something that's complex, doesn't work, and won't hold your team's

COMPASS POINT:

You are not trying to manage the sale.
You are trying to manage the activity.

attention. Don't try to reinvent the wheel! Remember: you are not trying to manage the sale – which is, let's face it, probably impossible. You're trying to manage the activity.

I'd love to hear your questions, insights, and experiences about implementing the STORM System. Please visit me at www.stormmethod. com – and stay in touch!

INDEX

Get Thirty Free Days Of On-Line Support For You ... And Your Sales Team ... As You Implement The Storm System!

Readers of this book, and all salespeople who report to them, are entitled to a FREE thirty-day subscription to the on-line STORM PLANNING support tool.

This is a simple tracking tool that is designed specifically to help teams implement the STORM System. It complements your existing pipeline management approach, and is easy to learn. E-mail tech support is included within your organization's FREE thirty-day trial.

To redeem your 30 days of FREE support as your team puts the powerful ideas you've learned in this book into practice ...

VISIT: www.StormMethod.com
ENTER THE USERNAME: StormReader
ENTER THE PASSWORD: StormReader

You'll be prompted from there.

Note: The fields are case-sensitive.

ABOUT SCOTT McLOUGHLIN

Founder and creator of the STORM Selling System

www.StormMethod.com

609-279-1911

smcloughlin@att.net

*S*cott McLoughlin has more than 25 years of successful sales and management experience in fields as diverse as media, energy, training and development, management consulting, information technology services, enterprise software and Internet technology. Scott has a unique blend of skills that includes setting the sales direction for "turnaround" situations, start-up companies, and large Fortune 500 corporations. He has held senior sales and management positions at Associated Press, Computer Task Group and Polaroid Graphic Imaging, as well as at start-up companies. He was hired early in his technology career by venture capitalist Ben Rosen of Sevin Rosen Management.

Scott has vast experience in working with Business-to-Business (B2B) clients who want to develop their sales force. He brings relevant experience to a wide range of clients including manufacturers, distributors and service organizations. He focuses on achieving performance improvements through targeted sales skills training, developing inside and field sales teams, structured involvement of sales management and executives and sales process improvement.

His successful sales management track record includes expertise in the field of petroleum products; he currently serves as Outsourced VP of Sales for several major petroleum & lubricants distributors. Scott has worked with hundreds of petroleum and lubricant reps around the

United States and Canada, delivering effective sales training programs. He recently developed "The Complete Sales Manager Program," which is being rolled out by Exxon Mobil worldwide.

Scott McLoughlin is well versed in strategic planning, creating, segments and growing markets. He also has experience in key account planning and opportunity management. He served as Director of Printing Technology Management at Drexel University's College of Media, Art, Architecture & Design.